#struggles

Also by Craig Groeschel

Altar Ego: Becoming Who God Says You Are

Chazown: A Different Way to See Your Life

*The Christian Atheist: Believing in God
but Living as If He Doesn't Exist*

Dare to Drop the Pose
(previously titled *Confessions of a Pastor*)

Fight: Winning the Battles That Matter Most

*From This Day Forward: Five Commitments
to Fail-Proof Your Marriage*
(with Amy Groeschel)

Love, Sex, and Happily Ever After
(previously titled *Going All the Way*)

*It: How Churches and Leaders
Can Get It and Keep It*

Soul Detox: Pure Living in a Polluted World

Weird: Because Normal Isn't Working

What Is God Really Like?
(general editor)

STUDY GUIDE   FIVE SESSIONS

#struggles

Following
Jesus in
a Selfie-
Centered
World

Craig Groeschel

with Christine M. Anderson

ZONDERVAN®

ZONDERVAN

#Struggles Study Guide
Copyright © 2015 by Craig Groeschel

This title is also available as a Zondervan ebook. Visit www.zondervan.com/ebooks.

Requests for information should be addressed to:

Zondervan, 3900 *Sparks Dr. SE, Grand Rapids, Michigan 49546*

ISBN 978-0-310-68485-5

Craig Groeschel is represented by Thomas J. Winters of Winters & King, Inc., Tulsa, Oklahoma.

Cover design: Dual Identity
Cover photography: © svetikd / *iStockphoto*®
Interior design: Denise Froehlich

First Printing August 2015 / Printed in the United States of America

QG 12-D2-16

Contents

How to Use This Guide

Group Size

The #*Struggles* video study is designed to be experienced in a group setting such as a Bible study, Sunday school class, or any small group gathering. To ensure everyone has enough time to participate in discussions, it is recommended that large groups break up into smaller groups of four to six people each.

Materials Needed

Each participant should have his or her own study guide, which includes notes for video segments, directions for activities and discussion questions, as well as personal studies to deepen learning between sessions.

Timing

The time notations—for example (17 minutes)—indicate the *actual* time of video segments and the *suggested* times for each activity or discussion. For example:

> **Individual Activity: What I Want to Remember (2 minutes)**

Adhering to the suggested times will enable you to complete each session in one hour. If you have a longer meeting, you may wish to allow more time for discussion and activities. You may also opt to devote two meetings rather than one to each session. In addition to allowing discussions to be more spacious, this has the added advantage of allowing group members to read related chapters in the #*Struggles* book and to complete the personal study between meetings. In the second meeting, devote the time allotted for watching the video to discussing group members' insights and questions from their reading and personal study.

Practice

Each session ends with a suggested application activity for group members to complete between sessions. Although the activity is completed outside of the group meeting, it's a good idea to read through the practice before concluding the meeting to clarify any questions and to make sure everyone is on board.

Facilitation

Each group should appoint a facilitator who is responsible for starting the video and for keeping track of time during discussions and activities. Facilitators may also read questions aloud and monitor discussions, prompting participants to respond and ensuring that everyone has the opportunity to participate.

Personal Studies

Maximize the impact of the curriculum with additional study between group sessions. Every personal study includes reflection questions, Bible study, and a guided prayer activity. You'll get the most out of the study by setting aside about thirty minutes between sessions for personal study, as well as additional time to complete the weekly practice activities.

#1

recovering contentment

The Struggle with Comparisons

> All day long we are bombarded with messages that seek to persuade us of two things: that we are (or ought to be) discontented and that contentment is only one step away: "use me, buy me, eat me, wear me, try me, drive me, put me in your hair."
>
> John Ortberg, *Love Beyond Reason*

Welcome!

Welcome to Session 1 of *#Struggles*. If this is your first time together as a group, take a moment to introduce yourselves to each other before the group activity. Then let's begin!

Group Activity: Devices Out and Down (2 minutes)

The *#Struggles* study explores how things like new technology and social media can complicate age-old struggles such as comparison, envy, jealousy, greed, and a variety of addictions. The goal is to learn biblical values that can help us restore balance in our lives and address any unhealthy overreliance we might have on technology. As a starting point, try taking a break from technology for the duration of your group meeting.

1. Take out your phone, tablet, or any other electronic device you may have with you. Turn it off or place it in airplane mode. (The only exception here and in all remaining sessions is for those who are using an ebook version of the guide and need their device to participate in the study. If so, put the device in airplane mode and use it only to access the guide.)

2. Set your device face down in the center of the room (if you are sitting in a circle), or at the front of the room (if you are sitting in rows). Ideally, you should be able to see your device but not be able to reach it.

3. Continue with the remainder of the group meeting. Rest assured that you *will* retrieve your device after closing prayer at the end of the session!

Video: Recovering Contentment (10 minutes)

Play the video segment for Session 1. As you watch, use the outline provided to follow along or to take additional notes on anything that stands out to you.

Notes

The more we compare, the less satisfied we are.

On social media, everybody else's life looks perfect. They're showing us their highlight reels, and we're comparing it with our behind-the-scenes.

More than one third of students felt significantly worse after spending time on Facebook. The number one emotion they felt was envy.

Chuck Swindoll: "Life is 10 percent what happens to you, and 90 percent how you respond." For so many of us, it is the exact opposite. It's all about what happens to us, and we forget that our response has any real value at all.

Here are three ways we can respond when we are tempted to compare and be envious:

1. *We will kill comparisons.* c̄ Christ's strength

   "But if you harbor bitter envy and selfish ambition in your hearts, do not boast about it or deny the truth. Such 'wisdom' does not come down from heaven but is earthly, unspiritual, demonic. For where you have envy and selfish ambition, there you find disorder and every evil practice" (James 3:14–16).

   Envy: Earthly, unspiritual + demonic

2. *We will celebrate other people's blessings.* thru Christ's power

   we will "Rejoice with those who rejoice; mourn with those who mourn" (Romans 12:15).

3. *We will cultivate gratitude.*

    Envy is resenting God's goodness in other people's lives and ignoring his goodness in your own.

    "Enjoy what you have rather than desiring what you don't have. Just dreaming about nice things is meaningless—like chasing the wind" (Ecclesiastes 6:9 NLT).

    "I know what it is to be in need, and I know what it is to have plenty. I have learned the secret of being content in any and every situation, whether well fed or hungry, whether living in plenty or in want. I can do all this through him who gives me strength" (Philippians 4:12–13).

When Christ is all you have, you'll recognize that Christ is all you need.

Group Discussion (46 minutes)

Take time to talk about what you just watched.

1. What part of the teaching had the most impact on you?

Living in a Selfie-Centered World

2. At the beginning of the video, Craig described how social media often leads us to compare our behind-the-scenes with everyone else's highlight reels. On Instagram, he saw friends attending a conference he wished he could attend, hanging out with people he wished he knew, vacationing in places he wished he could be. When

he compared where his friends were with where he was—stuck in his office—he felt discontent and bad about himself.

- Briefly describe a recent "highlight reel" you came across. How did it compare to your "behind-the-scenes"? What response did it prompt in you? For example: discontent, gratitude, envy, happiness, etc.

- Consider your own social media highlight reels. If someone you didn't know were to look at your last several posts on social media, would they be more likely to get the impression that your life is better than it really is, worse than it really is, or pretty close to how it actually is? Describe any examples that illustrate your response. (And no, you may not retrieve your device to illustrate your response!)

- Aside from social media, what else tends to trigger discontent or envy in you? For example: when someone you know gets a new car/gadget/outfit, has a great marriage or romantic relationship, has more favorable life circumstances, etc. In what ways, if any, do these experiences or your response to them differ from those triggered by social media?

3. A selfie-centered world is a world that makes everything about us. But if we want to live in a way that honors Christ—who calls us to die to ourselves and follow him—we have to be different. We have to resist the distractions, habits, and temptations that pull us away from loving God and loving others.

- Consider first how you are affected when a friend or family member uses technology or social media. How does their use of these tools strengthen your relationship or demonstrate their love and care for you? How does their use of these tools weaken your relationship or become a source of tension?

- Now consider how your own use of technology and social media impacts your relationships. In what ways are they tools that help you to love God and love others? In what ways are they distractions, habits, or temptations that pull you away from loving God and loving others?

Three Strategies for Battling Envy and Learning Contentment

4. Craig quoted pastor Chuck Swindoll as saying, "Life is 10 percent what happens to you, and 90 percent how you respond." Although we can't always stop the distractions and temptations that bombard us in a selfie-centered world, we can choose how we respond to them. As time permits, discuss one or more of the three strategies for battling envy: kill comparisons, celebrate other people's blessings, and cultivate gratitude.

Kill comparisons. We need to kill the comparisons that lead to envy because they are more serious than most of us realize. The apostle James puts it bluntly:

> But if you harbor bitter envy and selfish ambition in your hearts, do not boast about it or deny the truth. Such "wisdom" does not come down from heaven but is earthly, unspiritual, demonic. For where you have envy and selfish ambition, there you find disorder and every evil practice.

(James 3:14–16)

- Based on James's description, how would you assess the spiritual threat level envy poses? Choose a number on the continuum below and share the reasons for your response.

1   2   3   4   5   6   7   8   9   10
Envy is harmless.   **Envy is lethal.**

- What similarities or differences are there between how James describes envy and how you have tended to view the threat level it poses in your own life? For example, would you have chosen a smaller or larger number on the continuum to describe the level of threat envy poses to you? Why?

- One way to kill comparisons is to identify what triggers them and stop doing it. For example, we might hide a person's Facebook posts, unfollow them on Instagram or Twitter, turn off notifications, delete the app, or take a break from social media for a while. Beyond social media, we might throw out the catalogs, stop watching HGTV, cancel the annual trip to the boat show, or remove ourselves from whatever it is that leads to comparison and envy.

  If you were to take the spiritual threat level of envy as seriously as James does, what kinds of things might you have to stop doing?

Celebrate other people's blessings. When you see someone else being blessed in a way you hope to be blessed, choosing to celebrate with them can purify the intentions of your heart. The biblical principle is to:

Rejoice with those who rejoice; mourn with those who mourn.

(Romans 12:15)

- Briefly reflect on a time when someone authentically rejoiced and celebrated with you. What did that person say or do—not say or do—that made their response especially meaningful?

- What insights or principles are there in the experience you just described that might help you to celebrate other people's blessings in a way that is meaningful to them?

Cultivate gratitude. If envy is resenting God's goodness in other people's lives and ignoring God's goodness in your own, one way to battle envy is to train your heart to continually look for God's goodness. King Solomon, the richest man of all time, put it this way:

> Enjoy what you have rather than desiring what you don't have. Just dreaming about nice things is meaningless—like chasing the wind.
>
> (Ecclesiastes 6:9 NLT)

- In what area of life are you most tempted to "chase the wind," to focus on what you don't have rather than enjoying what you do have?

- If instead, you were to look for God's goodness in this area of life, what would you see that you could be authentically grateful for?

Strength for the Battle

5. Craig stressed that we can battle envy in all these ways by following the example of the apostle Paul, who relied on Christ's power to learn and practice contentment:

    > I know what it is to be in need, and I know what it is to have plenty. I have learned the secret of being content in any and every situation, whether well fed or hungry, whether living in plenty or in want. I can do all this through him who gives me strength.

    >   (Philippians 4:12 – 13)

    Earlier in his letter to the Philippians, Paul describes the source of this kind of strength:

    > I want to know Christ and experience the mighty power that raised him from the dead. I want to suffer with him, sharing in his death, so that one way or another I will experience the resurrection from the dead!

    >   (Philippians 3:10 – 11 NLT)

    Paul links Christ's power — the source of strength he needs to practice contentment — to sharing in Christ's death and resurrection. It's been said that nothing that has not died can be resurrected. In other words, we won't experience the power of new life and growth without first surrendering to some kind of loss or "death."

    *   In what ways do you feel like you lack the spiritual strength or power you need in order to let go of envy and experience contentment?

    *   What is it you might need to die to in order to experience the power of Christ in this weakness? How would you describe the "resurrection" or new life you hope to experience as a result?

6. At the start of the session you had a chance to begin practicing contentment by setting aside your phone or other electronic device. How has this brief separation from your device impacted you? For example: in what you thought about, in your ability to be present in the group, in raising awareness of how you rely on your device.

Friend Request

7. In addition to exploring *#Struggles* together as a group, it's important to also be aware of how God is at work among you—especially in how you relate to each other and share your lives throughout the study. In each session, there will be many opportunities to speak life-giving—and life-challenging—words and to listen to one another deeply.

As you anticipate the next several weeks of learning together in community, what request would you like to make of the group? For example, how do you hope other members will challenge you or encourage you? Use one or more of the sentence starters below, or your own statement, to help the group understand the best way to be a good friend to you throughout this study. As each person responds, use the two-page chart that follows to briefly note what is important to that person and how you can be a good friend to them during your discussions and times together.

I'd like you to consistently challenge me about . . .

It really helps me to engage in a group when . . .

I tend to withdraw or feel anxious when . . .

You can help me to take this study seriously by . . .

In our discussions, the best thing you could do for me is . . .

Name	The Best Way I Can Be a Good Friend to This Person Is ...
Charlene	Help c̄ judgementless + critical thinking.
Yoli	Make a difference in this World.
Robyn	critical thinker - judgemental.

(cont.)

Name	The Best Way I Can Be a Good Friend to This Person Is ...

Individual Activity: What I Want to Remember (2 minutes)

Complete this activity on your own.

1. Briefly review the outline and any notes you took.

2. In the space below, write down the most significant thing you gained in this session—from the teaching, activities, or discussions.

   What I want to remember from this session ...

   Few issues = envy - But too self envalued Need to reach out for others.

Practice: iStrategize

Each session in the #*Struggles* study includes a practice for you to complete between sessions. Although the practice is completed on your own and outside of group time, it's a good idea to read through the practice description before concluding your meeting each week. In some cases, activities may require preparation or setting aside time each day to complete. To get the most out of the practice, it's important not to hurry or try to complete activities at the last minute.

The practice for this week is to act on one or more of the three strategies Craig described for battling envy. Here are options for ways to do that between now and your next group meeting:

❑ *Kill comparisons.* Identify one comparison/envy trigger and stop doing it. Choose something that will be a stretch or a challenge for you. For example, if social media is a trigger, before you go to bed tonight, you might create a post to let your friends know you're taking a break and then do it—fast from social media for twenty-four hours, several days, or a full week. For additional ideas, see the examples given in question 4.

❑ *Celebrate other people's blessings.* Identify one person who tends to trigger comparisons and envy in you. Commit to two things on their behalf:

(1) Use a journal or pad of paper to pray for this person every day—at least seven written prayers between now and your next group meeting. Thank God for the specific ways he's blessed this person; ask God to continue blessing him or her, and to change your heart so that you genuinely desire increased blessing for this person.

(2) Celebrate and affirm this person in a tangible way. Prayers may be private but celebration is relational. When you celebrate someone, you seek to honor them in a meaningful way. For example, you might identify a personal trait you admire and tell them why you respect and appreciate that in them; note an accomplishment and congratulate them; identify a blessing they've experienced and affirm your gratitude for God's goodness to them. If possible, do this in person, honoring them with your presence as well as your words.

❏ *Cultivate gratitude.* Go on a daily hunt for God's goodness in your life by keeping a gratitude list. Throughout the day or at the end of the day, write down at least ten things you're grateful for. Set a daily alert on your phone as a reminder (unless you're fasting completely from technology!). You might choose to focus on a specific area in which you're struggling with envy or to focus on gratitude in general. Either way, begin by hunting for God's goodness in the little joys or graces you might otherwise take for granted: *God, thank you for ... hot coffee first thing in the morning, the beautiful sound of my child's laughter, enough money to pay the bills this month, giving me the courage to apologize, a good night's sleep.* At the end of the week, you will have expressed gratitude for least seventy good gifts. Read through all seven lists and then write a prayer of thanksgiving, praising God for his relentless goodness in your life and asking him to help you make gratitude the lens through which you routinely look at life.

Place a check mark next to one or more of the three options you'll practice this week and share it with the group.

Whatever option(s) you choose, consider setting aside some time to write down a few notes and observations about your experience throughout the week. You'll have a chance to talk about your experiences at the start of Session 2.

Closing Prayer

Close your time together with prayer. Following prayer, you are free at last to retrieve your electronic devices!

#1

Personal Study

Read and Learn

Read the introduction and chapter 1 of the book #*Struggles*. Use the space below to note any insights or questions you want to bring to the next group session.

Study and Reflect

> While I can't speak for you, I'm finally willing to admit the truth. I'm tethered to my phone, addicted to my favorite apps, and hooked on social media. Technology has become central to my life. I don't really control it. It controls me. And I don't like that.
>
> #*Struggles*, page 17

1. The purpose of the *#Struggles* study is to explore how things like new technology and social media can complicate age-old struggles we all have, and then to learn biblical values that can help us to address them. To get a feel for your starting point on this journey, use the questions that follow to briefly assess where you are right now. For each statement, circle the number on the continuum that best describes your response.

    a. I sometimes feel like a loser when I ~~look at social media~~. *Read*

        1   2   3   4   (5)   6   7   8   9   10
        Not at all   **Moderately**   **Completely**
        true of me.   **true of me.**   **true of me.**

    b. Looking at social media often triggers comparison and envy in me.

        1   2   3   4   5   6   7   8   9   10
        Not at all   **Moderately**   **Completely**
        true of me.   **true of me.**   **true of me.**

    c. I feel down or disappointed if I don't get an immediate response or a certain number of Likes on a social media post.

        1   2   3   4   5   6   7   8   9   10
        Not at all   **Moderately**   **Completely**
        true of me.   **true of me.**   **true of me.**

    d. My use of technology or social media has caused problems in one or more of my relationships.

        1   2   3   4   5   6   7   8   9   10
        Not at all   **Moderately**   **Completely**
        true of me.   **true of me.**   **true of me.**

    e. When I'm having a conversation with a friend face-to-face, it's normal for me to periodically check my phone or take a call.

        1   2   3   4   5   6   7   8   9   10
        Not at all   **Moderately**   **Completely**
        true of me.   **true of me.**   **true of me.**

    f. I have plenty of online followers and friends, but it's sometimes hard to find anyone to spend time with in real life.

        1   2   3   4   5   6   7   8   9   10
        Not at all   **Moderately**   **Completely**
        true of me.   **true of me.**   **true of me.**

g. I use technology or social media to avoid awkward social situations or face-to-face conversations.

1	2	3	4	5	6	7	8	9	10
Not at all true of me.				**Moderately true of me.**				**Completely true of me.**	

h. Most of the time, my real life is not what it appears to be on social media.

1	2	3	4	5	6	7	8	9	10
Not at all true of me.				**Moderately true of me.**				**Completely true of me.**	

i. I have made choices about how to spend my time based on whether or not the activity has potential to create a social media moment.

1	2	3	4	5	6	7	8	9	10
Not at all true of me.				**Moderately true of me.**				**Completely true of me.**	

j. The more I see pain and world crises in my social media feeds, the harder it is for me to feel compassion when I'm exposed to it.

1	2	3	4	5	6	7	8	9	10
Not at all true of me.				**Moderately true of me.**				**Completely true of me.**	

k. I express compassion and support for causes by Liking or reposting but rarely take action to respond beyond social media.

1	2	3	4	5	6	7	8	9	10
Not at all true of me.				**Moderately true of me.**				**Completely true of me.**	

l. I feel isolated or anxious without my phone.

1	2	3	4	5	6	7	8	9	10
Not at all true of me.				**Moderately true of me.**				**Completely true of me.**	

m. The first and last thing I do every day is check my phone (or other electronic device).

1	2	3	4	5	6	7	8	9	10
Not at all true of me.				**Moderately true of me.**				**Completely true of me.**	

n.   I sometimes lose sleep because of my engagement with technology or social media.

1   2   3   4   5   6   7   8   9   10
Not at all   Moderately   Completely
true of me.   true of me.   true of me.

o.   I would risk physical harm to retrieve my phone (or other electronic device) if it were lost or stolen.

1   2   3   4   5   6   7   8   9   10
Not at all   Moderately   Completely
true of me.   true of me.   true of me.

Transfer the numbers you circled for each of the questions to the blank chart. Add all the numbers and write the total in the space provided. Divide the total by 15 to determine your overall #struggles score.

Example

My Responses		My Responses	
a.	5	a.	_____
b.	4	b.	_____
c.	9	c.	_____
d.	5	d.	_____
e.	9	e.	_____
f.	6	f.	_____
g.	3	g.	_____
h.	3	h.	_____
i.	5	i.	_____
j.	6	j.	_____
k.	2	k.	_____
l.	5	l.	_____
m.	10	m.	_____
n.	6	n.	_____
o.	4	o.	_____
Total	82	Total	_____

$82 \div 15 = 5.4$

_____ ÷ 15 = _____

My total   My #struggles
score

My total   My #struggles
score

Finally, plot your #struggles score on the continuum below by marking it with an X. For example, an X between 5 and 6 would represent the 5.4 score from the example.

1	2	3	4	5	6	7	8	9	10

I rarely have struggles related to technology and social media.

I sometimes have struggles related to technology and social media.

I routinely have struggles related to technology and social media.

What is your initial response to your overall #struggles score? For example, in what ways does it seem accurate or inaccurate to you?

Briefly review your responses to the fifteen questions and circle two or three you rated closest to 10. What is the deeper *need*, *desire*, or *fear* that might be behind those statements? For example, a habit of checking one's phone at the beginning and end of the day might reflect a need for affirmation, a desire for relational connection, or a fear of missing out.

In what ways, if any, have these unmet needs, desires, or fears left you feeling discontent with some area of your life or potentially vulnerable to envy?

It's arguable that no generation before us has struggled with discontent as much as ours. Although we still have poverty and economic inequality, the everyday lives of most of us are filled with convenience, opportunity, and abundance — sometimes to the point of excess. Yet it doesn't take much for us to feel as though we aren't getting everything we deserve and to face disappointment. Add social media and what do you get? Never before have so many people had so much and felt so dissatisfied.

#Struggles, page 28

2. Even if technology and social media aren't significant issues in our lives, most of us still struggle with some kind of discontent — which means envy is often just one short step away. The challenge is that we don't always recognize envy for what it really is. Author Os Guinness offers this penetrating definition of envy:

> Envy is not simply aspiration or ambition.... Envy enters when, seeing someone else's happiness or success, we feel ourselves called into question. Then, out of the hurt of our wounded self-esteem, we seek to bring the other person down to our level by word or deed. They belittle us by their success, we feel; we should bring them down to their deserved level, envy helps us feel. Full-blown envy, in short, is dejection plus disparagement plus destruction.[1]

Using this description of envy as a framework, reflect on the subtle or not-so-subtle ways envy might be a temptation for you. Listed below are three common categories of envy: financial/material, relational, and circumstantial. In each category, complete these sentence starters: *When I see ... I feel wounded or belittled ... I'm afraid ... I'm tempted to bring him/her/them down by ...*

Financial/material: Envy of others' possessions, vacations, resources, experiences, clothing, gadgets, etc.

> Example:
>
> *When I see* ... Sara talking about her latest international trip
>
> *I feel wounded or belittled* ... by my lack of funds and my boring life.
>
> *I'm afraid* ... I will never have the exciting, meaningful life I really want.
>
> *I'm tempted to bring him/her/them down by* ... changing the subject, ignoring her posts about the trip, or making comments like, "It must be nice to have enough extra money to travel."

When I see ...

I feel wounded or belittled ...

I'm afraid ...

I'm tempted to bring him/her/them down by ...

Relational: Envy of others' social circles, connections, calendar, personal qualities, romance, family, etc.

Example:

When I see ... Instagram posts of Mike coaching his kids' soccer games

I feel wounded or belittled ... about my inability to spend more time with my kids.

I'm afraid ... of missing out on my kids' lives and of not being a good dad.

I'm tempted to bring him/her/them down by ... making sarcastic comments on his posts and giving him a hard time about how he "never works" when I see him at church.

When I see ...

I feel wounded or belittled ...

I'm afraid ...

I'm tempted to bring him/her/them down by ...

Circumstantial: Envy of others' lifestyle, opportunities, advantages, season of life, career, education, etc.

Example:

When I see ... a pregnant woman

I feel wounded or belittled ... by my inability to have a baby of my own.

I'm afraid ... I will never have the family I really want.

I'm tempted to bring him/her/them down by ... mentally belittling her and inventing or magnifying her faults—she is insensitive to women who can't conceive; she doesn't take care of herself; she won't be as good a mother as I would be; she takes her pregnancy for granted, etc.

When I see ...

I feel wounded or belittled ...

I'm afraid ...

I'm tempted to bring him/her/them down by ...

> We were created for more — much more. We were created not for earth but for eternity. We were created not to be liked but to show love. We were created not to draw attention to ourselves but to give glory to God. We were created not to collect followers but to follow Christ.... Nothing on earth can ever satisfy the spiritual longing you feel inside, even if you could collect it all. Nothing.
>
> #*Struggles*, page 20, 32–33

3. Briefly review your responses to question 2, focusing especially on your responses to "I'm afraid ..." What would you say is the spiritual longing behind these things you want but are afraid you may never have? For example, in what ways might God be present in these desires or be the source of these desires?

Contentment requires trust — trust that regardless of our circumstances, God is good and God is enough. It's not something that comes naturally to most of us, but like the apostle Paul, we can choose to learn and practice it.

> I know what it is to be in need, and I know what it is to have plenty.
> I have learned the secret of being content in any and every situation, whether well fed or hungry, whether living in plenty or in want.
> I can do all this through him who gives me strength.
> (Philippians 4:12–13)

For a fresh perspective on this familiar passage, read it again from *The Message*:

> I've learned by now to be quite content whatever my circum-stances. I'm just as happy with little as with much, with much as with little. I've found the recipe for being happy whether full or hungry, hands full or hands empty. Whatever I have, wherever I am, I can make it through anything in the One who makes me who I am.

> (Philippians 4:12–13 MSG)

What makes it difficult for you to trust God with your desires — to trust that God is good and God is enough regardless of your circumstances?

4. The psalms are sometimes referred to as the prayer book of the Bible. They not only teach us how to communicate with God, but they also help us to express things that are sometimes hard to put into words. Read Psalm 73, which is a prayer that acknowledges the pain of human envy and affirms the truth of God's goodness. Drawing on the psalm as a reference, use the space below to write your own

prayer. Acknowledge your doubts, questions, and areas where you are vulnerable to envy. Surrender your desires to God, asking him to help you learn contentment as you wait and to help you trust him with what's most important to you. Thank him for his goodness in your life just as it is right now.

#2

restoring intimacy

The Struggle with "Likes"

> To be present is to listen and to identify with each other as mortal, fragile human beings who need to be heard and sustained by one another, not distracted or entertained.
>
> Deirdre LaNoue, *The Spiritual Legacy of Henri Nouwen*

Group Activity: Devices Out and Away (2 minutes)

Welcome to Session 2 of #*Struggles*. In this session, we'll take a closer look at how technology and social media impact our relationships. To begin, you'll build on the practice you started last week of separating yourself from your electronics for the duration of your group meeting. Only this time, instead of placing devices in the center or front of the room where you can see them, you'll place them out of sight.

1. Take out your phone, tablet, or any other electronic device you may have with you. Turn it off or place it in airplane mode.

2. Choose a container such as a small box, basket, or a shopping bag and have everyone place their devices in the container. Place the container out of sight—in a cabinet, closet, or nearby room.

3. Continue with the remainder of the group meeting. Retrieve your devices after closing prayer at the end of the meeting.

Group Discussion: Checking In (10 minutes)

Check in with each other about what you've learned and experienced since the last session. For example:

- Briefly share your experience of the Session 1 practice activity you chose. What did you learn or experience in your efforts to battle envy?

- What insights did you discover in the personal study or in the chapter you read from the #*Struggles* book?

- How did the last session impact your daily life or your relationship with God?

- What questions would you like to ask the other members of your group?

Video: Restoring Intimacy (10 minutes)

Play the video segment for Session 2. As you watch, use the outline provided to follow along or to take additional notes on anything that stands out to you.

Notes

Too much use of technology will not only hurt your relationship with God, but it will hurt your relationships with others and distract you from what matters most.

"A new command I give you: Love one another. As I have loved you, so you must love one another. By this everyone will know that you are my disciples, if you love one another" (John 13:34–35).

Three ways that technology is changing relationships:

1. *The term "friend" is evolving.*

   The average adult Facebook user has 328 "friends."

   The average American only has what they would describe as two close friends.

   Twenty-five percent of Americans say that they have no close friends at all.

   We have more online activity but more limited personal intimacy.

2. *We are becoming addicted to immediate affirmation.*

   Instant gratification stimulates the brain's reward center, releasing a chemical called dopamine, and our brains can't get enough.

   Experts are saying that when people feel a little bit lonely, they post something. They get immediate affirmation but the reality is, they're actually deferring loneliness. They want someone to bring meaning to their lives, but all they get is a Like.

3. *We have the power to do friendship on our own terms.*

    If you text me, I have the power to respond or not.

    I can comment, I can follow you, or I can unfollow you.

    People say, "I've got all this online interaction. But the more I use social media, I actually crave more personal interaction."

    "I am more connected than ever before, and yet I feel more alone than ever before."

What do we do when we're very connected but something is missing? We can practice the power of presence.

"And let us not neglect our meeting together, as some people do, but encourage one another" (Hebrews 10:25 NLT).

There is something powerful that happens when we come together with other people.

Immanuel means "God with us."

God didn't shout his love from heaven. He showed his love on earth.

"Don't just pretend to love others. Really love them.... Love each other with genuine affection, and take delight in honoring each other.... When God's people are in need, be ready to help them" (Romans 12:9–10, 13 NLT).

Two ways to practice the power of presence:

1. *Be present. Spend time with people face-to-face.*

    What's acceptable today is to send a text message. What's better is to pick up the phone and call them. What's even better than that is to see them—to go and be present.

    "For where two or three gather in my name, there am I with them" (Matthew 18:20).

    There is a big difference between just praying *for* somebody and praying *with* them.

2. *Be emotionally engaged.*

    We're having a conversation and our phone buzzes, and we just look away and we're engaged with somebody else. Be engaged with the person who is in front of you.

    At the end of your life, what matters is not going to be how many Likes you got but how much love you showed.

Connect all day long on technology, but when the time is right, put it down, get face-to-face, and love one another.

Group Discussion (36 minutes)

Take time to talk about what you just watched.

1.   What part of the teaching had the most impact on you?

Technology Is Changing Relationships

As time permits, discuss one or more of the following three questions about how technology is changing relationships.

2.   There are many ways in which technology and social media can enhance and support relationships. However, in order to use these tools well, we must also acknowledge the ways in which use or over-use might hurt relationships or distract us from what's most important. Briefly review the list of statements that follow. Place a check mark next to any statements you relate to, or write in your own statement below.

❑   The more I use social media, the more I crave personal interaction.

❑   I'm linked to dozens or hundreds of people online, but I often feel detached from interpersonal relationships.

❑   I sometimes wonder if social media is replacing my relationships more than enhancing them.

❑   The more I dabble in social media, the more I realize I'm delaying the personal interaction I really want.

❑   Once when I was going through a difficult time, I was hurt or disappointed that a friend sent me an email, a text, or a comment rather than reaching out for a real conversation.

❑   Sometimes when I get together with friends, they're so distracted by their phones that I end up feeling more alone than if I'd stayed home by myself.

❑   I've sometimes ruined or missed out on real-life moments with people I care about by trying to capture, manufacture, or post a social media moment.

❑   Other: _____

_____

Of the statements you checked, which do you relate to most? Share the reasons for your response.

3. Craig described how the immediate affirmation we get from a social media post could give us a sense of relational connection in the short term, but in reality we might simply be "deferring loneliness." In other words, not only are we not meeting our need for connection, we're deepening and prolonging our isolation.

   • Do you think it's possible to experience face-to-face the kind of immediate affirmation we get from social media responses? Why or why not?

   • Briefly compare the experience of affirmation you might get from real-life relationships or face-to-face conversations with the affirmation you get from Likes, retweets, and comments, etc. For example, in what ways might each kind of affirmation address or fail to address loneliness? How is each satisfying or dissatisfying? More or less meaningful? Easier or harder to give?

   • Which of the following statements do you resonate with more? Share the reasons for your response.

     The experience of immediate affirmation in social media puts unrealistic expectations and pressure on real-time relationships and face-to-face interactions.

     The hunger for immediate affirmation in social media is a sign that we need to be more proactive and generous with affirmation in real-time relationships and face-to-face interactions.

4. Technology and social media give us a unique power to do relationships on our own terms, especially in how we give or withhold approval, access, and information. For example, we can communicate a lot by whether or not we ... follow or unfollow; Like or don't Like; comment or don't comment; answer or let it go to voice mail; respond immediately, later, or not at all. In what we post about ourselves, we have the ability to control everything others see and know about us—including our appearance, personality, and lifestyle.

We all exercise some kind of control over our relationships, including setting healthy boundaries and living by relational values that are important to us. However, we've probably also experienced what it's like when someone—who may in fact be us—goes too far and is controlling in a way that inhibits or damages a relationship.

- When it comes to technology and social media, how would you distinguish between the two kinds of control? In other words, at what point does this power to do relationships on our own terms stunt our relational skills or damage our relationships? As part of your response, share any examples you can think of.

- How do you recognize this need to do relationships on our own terms *outside* of technology and social media? For example, how do we tend to give and withhold approval of others, and give or withhold access and information about ourselves in real-time relationships and interactions?

- What, if anything, distinguishes the controlling behaviors we use in real time from those we use with technology and social media?

Practicing the Power of Presence

5. Craig described the power of presence—of spending time together face-to-face and being emotionally engaged. The apostle Paul gives us a picture of what it might look like in practical terms to love people in this way:

> Don't just pretend to love others. Really love them.... Love each other with genuine affection, and take delight in honoring each other.... When God's people are in need, be ready to help them. Always be eager to practice hospitality.

(Romans 12:9–10, 13 NLT)

For a fresh perspective on this passage, read it again from *The Voice*:

> Love others well, and don't hide behind a mask; love authentically.... Live in true devotion to one another, loving each other as sisters and brothers. Be first to honor others by putting them first.... Share what you have with the saints, so they lack nothing; take every opportunity to open your life and home to others.

(Romans 12:9–10, 13 The Voice)

* Paul describes several actions that elaborate on what it means to "love others well." As you review the passage, which actions stand out as something you wish you could experience more—either on the giving or the receiving end?

* The fact that you are meeting together for this study is an indication that you are already practicing the power of presence. What would you say is the next challenge for your group? In other words, how can you be even more intentional about being engaged when you are together?

6. A recent study published in the *Journal of Social and Personal Relationships* revealed that the mere presence of a mobile phone nearby can diminish the quality of relational connection between two people in conversation.[2]

    At the start of this gathering, you had a chance to practice being present and engaged by putting your phones or other electronic devices out of sight. During the last session, you put your devices down but kept them in sight. What difference, if any, did having your devices out of sight make in your ability to be present this week?

7. At the end of the Session 1 group discussion, you had the opportunity to make a request of the group and to write down the best ways you could be good friends to one another.

    •   Briefly restate what you asked for from the group in Session 1. What additions or clarifications would you like to make that would help the group to know more about how to be a good friend to you? As each person responds, add any additional information to the Session 1 chart. (If you were absent from the last session, share your response to Session 1, question 7. Then use the chart to write down what is important to each member of the group.)

    •   In what ways, if any, did you find yourself responding differently to other members of the group in this session based on what they asked for in the previous session? What made that easy or difficult for you to do?

Individual Activity: What I Want to Remember (2 minutes)

Complete this activity on your own.

1. Briefly review the outline and any notes you took.

2. In the space below, write down the most significant thing you gained in this session—from the teaching, activities, or discussions.

   What I want to remember from this session ...

Practice: iEngage

The practice for this week is to love others well by practicing the power of presence and putting boundaries on technology. Choose one or more of the following options as your practice between now and the next group meeting.

❏ *Choose to be fully engaged.* Identify one or two people you routinely spend time with during the week (family, friends, colleagues, classmates, neighbors, etc.). Every time you are with them, give them your full attention. Put devices on silent and keep them out of sight, eliminate distractions (loud background music or television, etc.), and allow this individual to be the most important person in the world while you are together. Being fully engaged doesn't necessarily mean you have to have a long or soul-baring conversation, though there may be times when that will happen. Simply demonstrate a natural and genuine interest in the person you're with. Start with, "Hey, how are you doing?" Then listen attentively to what they say, noting their tone of voice and body language, which will also be communicating something. Cultivate a gentle curiosity by asking follow-up questions, be responsive to what they say, and see where the conversation takes you. Refuse to allow technology, other people, or anything else to distract you from being fully engaged with this person whenever you are together.

☐   *Create and follow ground rules for phone use.* Practice being present (to yourself and others) by setting boundaries on your phone use. For example:

- I will put my phone away and not look at it whenever I am in conversation with someone.

- I will put my phone away and not look at it during meals (whether I am eating with someone or eating alone).

- I will put my phone away and not look at it while attending social gatherings, entertainment events (concerts, movies, etc.), small group, class, or church.

- I will put my phone away at least thirty minutes before I go to bed, and not look at it while in bed.

- I will not multiscreen—if I'm enjoying a movie or television show, I will not simultaneously use my phone or laptop to do other things.

- I will not read or write text messages or otherwise check communications on my phone while driving (even when I am at a stoplight or in heavy traffic).

☐   *Post reposts or portraits only.* Devote your use of technology entirely to enhancing your relationships. If you routinely post to social media, instead of posting your own photos, tweets, or updates, devote your posts this week exclusively to reposting what others have posted. Honor them by adding an affirming comment about who they are or what they've written, photographed, or accomplished. If you're more into posting selfies, devote your posts instead entirely to portraits of others. Use a hashtag like #hihaveyoumet and describe in detail what you enjoy, admire, or respect about the person in the portrait.

Place a check mark next to one or more of the three options you'll practice this week and share it with the group.

Whatever option(s) you choose, consider setting aside some time to write down a few notes and observations about your experience throughout the week. You'll have a chance to talk about your experiences at the start of Session 3.

Closing Prayer

Close your time together with prayer. Following prayer, retrieve your electronic devices.

#2

Personal Study

Read and Learn

Read chapter 2 of #*Struggles*. Use the space below to note any insights or questions you want to bring to the next group session.

Study and Reflect

> We should maximize all that technology offers to help strengthen our friendships and relationships. But as the gravitational pull to live online continues to grow, we must remind ourselves that the best relationships are not those that are limited to looking at a screen but those that involve loving a person in person.
>
> #*Struggles*, page 209

1. Think back to the last few times you were together with a friend or a group of friends or family. In what ways, if any, did you use technology while you were together? Check all that apply.

❑   I took a phone call.

❑   I made a phone call.

❑   I checked my phone because I was bored.

❑   I checked my phone because the conversation felt awkward or uncomfortable.

❑   I checked my phone because ... that's what I do!

❑   I excused myself to use the bathroom as a cover so I could check my phone without anyone knowing.

❑   I checked my phone by stealth, hiding it behind or beneath something.

❑   I kept my phone out and face up on the table so I could glance at notifications.

❑   I texted someone else.

❑   I took photos of something besides the people I was with as a way to redirect or step out of the conversation.

❑   I took photos of the people I was with and then spent time editing and/or posting rather than being with them.

❑   When someone I was with had a question, I suggested looking it up on my phone as an excuse to also check my email/texts/social media.

❑   I listened to what others were saying in hopes of getting a tweet or a post out of the conversation.

❑   I tried to look like I was listening, but mentally I was already writing an update about what we were doing together.

☑   Other: _Showed photos of my_ _house to family group_

2. Based on the items you checked, how would you assess the degree to which you were present to the people you were with? Circle the number on the continuum that best describes your response.

1   2   3   4   5   6   7   8   (9)   10
I was barely   **I was completely**
present.   **present.**

What about the friends or family you were with? Based on their use of technology or level of distraction, how present were they to you and others?

1   2   3   4   5   6   7   8   (9)   10
I was barely   **I was completely**
present.   **present.**

In what ways, if any, might your time together have been different if none of you had accessed technology?

> Text away. Tweet what you're doing. Post what you're eating. But put more effort into your treasured relationships. . . . Don't just do life together from a distance. Do life up close.
>
> *#Struggles*, page 209

3. Author Jean Vanier, founder of L'Arche communities for people with disabilities, offers this compelling description of what it looks like to put effort into treasured relationships and to do life up close:

> To love someone is to show to them their beauty, their worth and their importance; it is to understand them, understand their cries and their body language; it is to rejoice in their presence, spend time in their company and communicate with them. To love is to live a heart-to-heart relationship with another, giving to and receiving from each other.[3]

When has someone put this kind of effort into their relationship with you? Use the sentence starters below for your response.

Jacqui (Name) showed me my beauty, worth, or importance by... *praying for me . Loving me*

_____ (Name) understood my cries and/or my body language when ...

_____ (Name) rejoiced in my presence when ...

Barb (Name) spent time with me, communicating with me when ... *we went to lunch*

_____ (Name) showed me how to live in a heart-to-heart relationship by ...

_____ (Name) taught me what it means to give and receive by ...

What insights do these experiences provide about what it means to be present to someone, to put effort into a relationship, to do life up close?

In what ways do these experiences challenge, motivate, or affirm your attempts to be present and put effort into your relationships?

Don't just be present; be all there. Engage deeply. Go all in. Make sure that the person you're with is the most important person in the world when you're together.

#Struggles, page 59

4. It's been said that the most important thing we will ever learn in life is to love and be loved. Jesus said that it requires being "all in" in order to love this way:

    "Love the Lord your God with *all* your heart and with *all* your soul and with *all* your mind and with *all* your strength.... [and] Love your neighbor as yourself. There is no commandment greater than these."

    (Mark 12:30–31, emphasis added)

The apostles Peter and John put it this way:

> Most important of all, continue to show deep love for each other.
>
> (1 Peter 4:8 NLT)

> Dear children, let's not merely say that we love each other; let us show the truth by our actions.
>
> (1 John 3:18 NLT)

If you were to take these verses seriously—to be all in—how would you respond?

Who do you sense God may be inviting you to engage deeply, to make the most important person in the world when you are together?

5. Read Psalm 136, a psalm that affirms God's loyal love and all the ways God has taken action to demonstrate his love. Drawing on the psalm as a reference, use the space below to write your own prayer. Acknowledge the ways God has acted on his loyal love for you, and thank him for his faithfulness. Ask him to lead and guide you as you continue to learn how to love and be loved.

#3

revealing authenticity

The Struggle with Control

> All of us have a secret desire to be seen as saints, heroes, martyrs. We are afraid to be children, to be ourselves.
>
> Jean Vanier, *Community and Growth*

Group Activity: Devices Out and Away (7 minutes)

Welcome to Session 3 of #*Struggles*. In this session, we'll consider how social media impacts our ability to be authentic. You'll also continue to build on the practice of separating yourself from your electronics for the duration of your group meeting. But first, you'll have a chance to actually use your devices in the group.

1. Take out your phone, tablet, or any other electronic device you may have with you. Open up your photos or a social media app where you post photos.

2. Choose a recent selfie to share with the group. If you don't have a selfie, choose a photo of yourself that you like that was taken by someone else. (Either way, it doesn't have to be a photo that you've posted.)

3. Briefly pass your device around the group to share your photo. (You'll have a chance to discuss the photos later in the meeting, so resist the temptation to comment on them now!)

4. When everyone has seen your photo, turn off your device or place it in airplane mode.

5. Choose a container such as a small box, basket, or a shopping bag and have everyone place their devices in the container. Place the container out of sight—in a cabinet, closet, or nearby room.

6. Continue with the remainder of the group meeting. Retrieve your devices after closing prayer at the end of the meeting.

Group Discussion: Checking In (5 minutes)

Check in with each other about what you've learned and experienced since the last session. For example:

- Briefly share your experience of the Session 2 practice activity you chose. What did you learn or experience in your efforts to be present and to put boundaries on technology?

- What insights did you discover in the personal study or in the chapter you read from the #*Struggles* book?

- How did the last session impact your daily life or your relationship with God?

- What questions would you like to ask the other members of your group?

Video: Revealing Authenticity (10 minutes)

Play the video segment for Session 3. As you watch, use the outline provided to follow along or to take additional notes on anything that stands out to you.

Notes

We live in a totally and completely selfie-obsessed world.

What we are trying to do is to show the world the "me" that I want them to see.

The more filtered our lives become, the less authentic we are.

One day we wake up and have all sorts of other struggles and don't know why.

We fear and avoid unfiltered communication.

Many people are afraid to have a conversation in real time because that conversation can't be edited.

"We are not like Moses, who would put a veil over his face to prevent the Israelites from seeing the end of what was passing away" (2 Corinthians 3:13).

What veil are you wearing? In what area of your life are you showing the world some me that you want them to see instead of the me that you really are?

Some people have been honest enough to admit that they try to think of doing things that are social media worthy—they're living their life to try to create a social media moment.

A veil that covers the face eventually covers the heart.

What started out as a superficial covering became a spiritual condition.

Today, there are many people who simply don't know how to open up.

We are so used to showing the fake self that we don't even know who the real self is.

We're living for Likes while at the same time longing for love.

We don't understand what brings connection. We may impress people with our strengths, but we connect with people through our weaknesses.

How to respond:

1. *Be yourself. Show yourself.*

   Take a social media break. Challenge yourself not to use filters. Be who you actually are.

   Christ can remove the veil.

   "But whenever anyone turns to the Lord, the veil is taken away" (2 Corinthians 3:16).

2. *Turn to God.*

   Instead of turning to everyone else for approval or for your identity, turn to God and suddenly, your identity is not in Likes but in his love.

"Where the Spirit of the Lord is, there is freedom. And we all, who with unveiled faces contemplate the Lord's glory, are being transformed into his image with ever-increasing glory" (2 Corinthians 3:17–18).

Group Discussion (36 minutes)

Take a few minutes to talk about what you just watched.

1. What part of the teaching had the most impact on you?

You and Your Selfie

2. On the video, Craig demonstrated various kinds of selfies. How would you characterize the selfie you shared with the group before you put your phone away? See the list below for examples. If you weren't able to access a photo to share, use the examples as a prompt to recall a recent selfie or other photo of you and share how you would characterize it.

- Cool selfie
- Surprised laugh selfie
- I-am-not-really-taking-this-photo-but-I-am selfie
- Driving in my car selfie
- Duck-face selfie
- Me and my #bff selfie
- Kissing somewhere cool selfie
- Me with my food selfie
- Mani/pedi selfie
- I'm rocking this outfit selfie
- I just woke up selfie
- New 'do selfie (for a new haircut)
- Me and my pet selfie
- Birthday selfie
- I did it! selfie
- I'm-on-vacay-and-you're-not selfie
- Me at the gym selfie
- Silly selfie
- Just my feet selfie
- Group selfie
- Support my cause selfie

3. Tell the group a little bit more about your selfie.

    - If you had to make an "I" statement based on your selfie, what would it be? For example, for a group selfie it might be, "I have a lot of friends" or "I have a great social life." For a silly selfie it might be, "I don't take myself too seriously." For the surprised laugh selfie, it might be, "I'm a good time!"

    - Craig pointed out that sometimes on social media we show the world a version of ourselves that filters out a larger truth. For example, a gym selfie with a protein shake might convey, "I'm getting in shape," when the larger truth is you also just ate a bag of chips and a gallon of ice cream. Is there a larger truth that's filtered out in the selfie you shared? If so, in what ways does it contradict your "I" statement (what the photo conveys)?

4. Whether it's on social media or in other contexts, we all face the temptation to create snapshot versions of ourselves to impress others or to manage how they see us. And yet the more we rely on these filtered or partial versions of ourselves to generate affirmation and acceptance, the harder it is to be authentic. Author and scholar Brené Brown defines authenticity in part as "cultivating the courage to be emotionally honest, to set boundaries, and to allow ourselves to be vulnerable. . . . We let go of what we are supposed to be and embrace who we are." [4]

    - Based on Brené Brown's definition, do you think it's possible to be authentic on social media? Share any examples you can think of to illustrate your response.

- If the filtered or partial version of who you are is what gets affirmed and accepted, what happens to the rest of who you are? How does this impact your ability to have authentic relationships?

- If social media trains us to present filtered and partial truths about ourselves, what relationships or contexts would you say train us in authenticity?

Veiled and Unveiled Faces

5. To illustrate the human tendency to hide or filter the truth about ourselves, Craig shared the story of how Moses once covered his face with a veil. To better understand the background and context for this story, read "Why Did Moses Wear a Veil?" (below). Go around the group and have a different person read aloud one or two paragraphs at a time. Then use the questions that follow to continue your discussion.

Why Did Moses Wear a Veil?

Moses had gone to the top of Mount Sinai where God gave him the Ten Commandments. He spent forty days on the mountain with God, and here's how the Bible describes what happened afterward:

> When Moses came down from Mount Sinai with the two tablets of the covenant law in his hands, he was not aware that his face was radiant because he had spoken with the LORD. When Aaron and all the Israelites saw Moses, his face was radiant, and they were afraid to come near him. But Moses called to them; so Aaron and all the leaders of the community came back to him, and he spoke to them. Afterward all the Israelites came near him, and he gave them all the commands the LORD had given him on Mount Sinai.

(cont.)

> When Moses finished speaking to them, he put a veil over his face. But whenever he entered the LORD's presence to speak with him, he removed the veil until he came out. And when he came out and told the Israelites what he had been commanded, they saw that his face was radiant. Then Moses would put the veil back over his face until he went in to speak with the LORD.
>
> (Exodus 34:29–35)

The text doesn't specify why Moses covered his face, so we might conclude from the passage that perhaps he used a veil to make it easier for people to approach him, to protect them from the fear-inspiring glory of God on his face. The apostle Paul, however, offers another explanation:

> We are not like Moses, who would put a veil over his face to prevent the Israelites from seeing the end of what was passing away. But their minds were made dull, for to this day the same veil remains when the old covenant is read. It has not been removed, because only in Christ is it taken away. Even to this day when Moses is read, a veil covers their hearts. But whenever anyone turns to the Lord, the veil is taken away. Now the Lord is the Spirit, and where the Spirit of the Lord is, there is freedom. And we all, who with unveiled faces contemplate the Lord's glory, are being transformed into his image with ever-increasing glory, which comes from the Lord, who is the Spirit.
>
> (2 Corinthians 3:13–18)

According to Paul, Moses wasn't trying to protect the people—he was trying to protect himself! He wanted to keep people from seeing that *the glory was fading*. Moses didn't want to be seen as anything less than radiant. He used the veil because he felt too insecure to be his ordinary, nonglowing self in front of others. Paul uses this example to show the Corinthians how much greater the new covenant (freedom through Christ) is than the old covenant (adherence to the law). He then makes a comparison. When the old covenant was read, the Jewish people who didn't believe in Christ could not see the truth. Why? Because their unbelief blinded them like a veil. But anyone who turns to Christ understands the truth, because he removes this veil and reveals God's glory. Paul wanted the Corinthians to know that that's when they become truly radiant, and not with a glory that fades, but with an "increasing glory" as they are transformed into the image of Christ.

- In what ways, if any, do you relate to Moses?

- What insecurities make it hard to be your ordinary self with others (on social media or otherwise)? What "veils" do you tend to use to cover those insecurities?

- Paul uses the veil as a metaphor to describe the spiritual impairment that blinded the Jewish people of his day to the truth about Jesus — he said a veil covered their hearts. Craig elaborated when he said, "A veil that covers the face eventually covers the heart. What started out as a superficial covering became a spiritual condition." How do you recognize this dynamic in connection with the veils or filters you and others use (on social media or otherwise)? In other words, how might these superficial coverings become spiritual impairments?

- How would you describe what it means to have an unveiled face? Consider this both in the spiritual context that Paul describes and in a relational context (the way we present ourselves to others).

- When Paul says that we "contemplate the Lord's glory," the Greek word he uses for "contemplate" can be literally translated "beholding as in a mirror."[5] It's a beautiful image. When we choose to gaze at Christ's glory (rather than our own), we not only increasingly reflect his glory, but we also begin to see the beauty of our unveiled faces reflected back to us—the "ever increasing glory" of the person God created us to be.

  What do you find challenging or compelling about this image of Christ's glory as a mirror?

  In what ways do you sense God may be inviting you to gaze into this mirror—to see yourself illuminated by the light of Christ?

6. Take a few moments to reflect on what you've learned and experienced together in this study so far.

   - How has learning more about struggles with social media impacted you and your relationship with God?

   - Since the first session, what shifts have you noticed in yourself in terms of how you relate to the group? For example, do you feel more or less guarded, understood, challenged, encouraged, connected, etc.?

- What adjustments, if any, would you like to make to the Session 1 chart that would help other members of the group know how to be a good friend to you?

Individual Activity: What I Want to Remember (2 minutes)

Complete this activity on your own.

1. Briefly review the outline and any notes you took.

2. In the space below, write down the most significant thing you gained in this session—from the teaching, activities, or discussions.

   What I want to remember from this session ...

Practice: *iUnveil*

The practice for this week is to pursue authenticity by setting aside the "veil" or filters you sometimes use to impress others or to manage how they see you. Choose one or both of the following options as your practice between now and the next group meeting.

❏ *Commit to simplicity of speech and action.* Identify a relationship or a group in which you are tempted to prop up your image—to say or do things in order to appear smart, spiritual, funny, successful, etc. Commit to simplicity of speech and action in these relationships by identifying six to eight things you will and will not do when you are with the person(s) you identified. For example:

- I will not name drop.

- I will not seek to attract attention to myself.

- I will not exaggerate.

- I will not massage the truth to make myself look better.

- I will not make comments about my accomplishments or talents.

- I will not perform tasks or actions motivated solely by a need to be recognized.

- I will not make self-deprecating remarks to manipulate others into praising or affirming me.

- I will not use flattery to manipulate others into liking me.

- I will not use put-downs or criticism of others to put myself in a more favorable light.

- I will promptly and humbly acknowledge faults or failures when appropriate.

- I will strive to be humbly and gently honest in everything I say and do.

- I will focus on God as the source of my identity and significance whenever I feel insecure.

Write down your commitments on a pad of paper or email them to yourself. Read and pray through them daily, asking God to help you lift the veil and experience the freedom of more authentic relationships.

❏ *Give your social media an authenticity assessment.* Briefly review your posts from the last few weeks. Write down two or three observations about the ways you subtly or not-so-subtly use images and words to impress others or to manage how they see you. For example, "I only post 'candids' of my kids when their clothes match and their hair is combed because I want people to see me as a good mom," or "I tend to tweet a lot of inspirational quotes because I want people to see my spiritual side." For each observation you write down, write a corresponding statement to challenge yourself to greater authenticity in your posts. For example, "I can post photos of my kids when they're a mess and still be a good mom," or "I can tweet news or humor that interests me without compromising my faith." Then use these statements to help you raise the authenticity quotient in your posts this week. For photos, use captions to acknowledge any "larger truths" (as discussed in question 3) that might not otherwise be evident. In whatever you write—comments, updates, tweets, captions—challenge yourself to be humbly and gently honest. Being authentic does not mean being brutally confrontational about everything on your mind—and you don't have to reveal everything. Just make sure that what you do write is a reflection of the real you.

Place a check mark next to one or both of the options you'll practice this week and share it with the group.

Whichever option(s) you choose, consider setting aside some time to write down a few notes and observations about your experience throughout the week. You'll have a chance to talk about your experiences at the start of Session 4.

Closing Prayer

Close your time together with prayer. Following prayer, retrieve your electronic devices.

#3

Personal Study

Read and Learn

Read chapter 3 of #*Struggles*. Use the space below to note any insights or questions you want to bring to the next group session.

Study and Reflect

> We are all filtering and editing our lives, and the more we do, the more difficulty we have being authentic.
>
> And if we can't be real, are we really living?
>
> #*Struggles*, page 74

1. At some point, all of us have a desire to be seen as "the 'me' I want to be"—a more impressive or accomplished version of ourselves. Use the list below to reflect on the "me" you want to be by placing a check mark next to the characteristics you resonate with most.

   The me I want to be is . . .

   ☐ *Wise:* I want to understand the deeper meaning of things in order to live well.

   ☑ *Responsible:* I want to be rock solid and reliable, a good person in every way.

   ☑ *Fun:* I want to bring joy and celebration to life.

   ☐ *Strong:* I want to have influence and change things for the better.

   ☑ *Easy going:* I want to be a relaxed and peaceful presence in the world.

   ☐ *Perfect:* I want my life to be whole and well ordered.

   ☑ *Helpful:* I want to meet needs and make a contribution to the world.

   ☐ *Successful:* I want to achieve and exceed my limitations.

   ☐ *Unique:* I want to do things differently and be creative in the way I live my life.

   ☐ Other: _____
   _____

   What kinds of subtle or obvious things are you likely to do or say to make sure that others see these characteristics in you? (Consider how you do this in social media as well as real-time relationships.)

What insecurities lie behind the characteristics you checked? In other words, what are you afraid will happen if you are *not* perceived by others to be wise, strong, or perfect, etc.?

In what ways has your need to protect these insecurities made it difficult for you to be authentic—emotionally honest and vulnerable—in your relationships?

The danger is that we can become so used to showing our filtered self, so accustomed to the half-truths and exaggerations, that we don't even know who our real self is anymore. Are you one person in one group of people and a different person in another group? Until you show who you really are, until you know and are fully known, you're going to be longing for something more.

#Struggles, page 81

2. In his book *Telling Secrets*, author and pastor Frederick Buechner writes compellingly about the importance of authenticity and self-disclosure:

> What we hunger for perhaps more than anything else is to be known in our full humanness, and yet that is often just what we also fear more than anything else. It is important to tell at least from time to time the secret of who we truly and fully are ... because otherwise we run the risk of losing track of who we truly and fully are and little by little come to accept instead the highly edited version which we put forth in hope that the world will find it more acceptable than the real thing. It is important to tell our secrets too because it makes it easier ... for other people to tell us a secret or two of their own, and exchanges like that ... have a lot to do with what being human is all about."[6]

In your life, how big is the gap between what Buechner describes as the "highly edited version" you put forth and the "real thing"? Is it a small gap, an enormous one, somewhere between? In what relationships or situations are you most aware of the gap?

What is it you feel the world would find unacceptable about the real thing—who you truly and fully are?

Vulnerability is always risky and frightening, but is there anything you find intriguing or compelling about what Buechner describes? What would you most like to experience if you could?

We want so badly to connect with others, and we think the best way to do so is by showing off our strengths. But that doesn't work. Here's why: We actually connect with people through our weaknesses. We may impress them with our strengths, but we connect through our weaknesses.

#Struggles, page 82

3. Briefly reflect back on your responses to question 1. In what ways, if any, might you have confused making an *impression* with making a *connection*? In other words, how have you hoped that being perceived in a certain way would help you to feel closer to others?

What invitation do you sense God may be extending to you in connection with your weaknesses?

4. Read Psalm 139, a prayer that expresses the wonder of being intimately known by God. Drawing on the psalm as a reference, use the space below to write your own prayer. Acknowledge the ways God knows you better than you know yourself and thank him for loving and accepting you just as you are. Share your insecurities and any fears you have about being more authentic in your relationships. Ask him for what you need from him as you take your next steps to know and be known.

resurrecting compassion

The Struggle with Desensitization

> Love is a do thing.
>
> Bob Goff, *Love Does*

Group Activity: Devices Out and Away (7 minutes)

Welcome to Session 4 of #*Struggles*. In this session, we'll consider how social media impacts our ability to be compassionate. You'll also continue to build on the practice of separating yourself from your electronics for the duration of your group meeting. But first, you'll use your devices in the group.

1. Take out your phone, tablet, or any other Internet-connected electronic device you may have with you and open up your Internet browser.

2. On your own, do a brief search for facts and statistics about suffering in the world, targeting *one* of the following topics:

Poverty	Homelessness	Mental illness
Domestic abuse	Human trafficking	Mass incarceration
Human rights abuses	Child soldiers	Water-related disease
Slavery	Refugees	Addiction
Armed conflict	Hunger or malnutrition	Religious persecution
Orphans	Racism	
Sexual violence	Child labor	

3. Write down one to three facts in the space below. You'll have a chance to discuss your facts after watching the video.

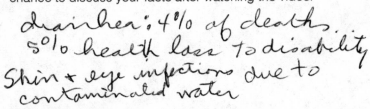

diarrhea: 4% of deaths,
5% health loss to disability
Skin + eye infections due to
contaminated water

4. Turn off your device or place it in airplane mode.

5. Choose a container such as a small box, basket, or a shopping bag and have everyone place their devices in the container. Place the container out of sight—in a cabinet, closet, or nearby room.

6. Continue with the remainder of the group meeting. Retrieve your devices after closing prayer at the end of the meeting.

Group Discussion: Checking In (5 minutes)

Check in with each other about what you've learned and experienced since the last session. For example:

- Briefly share your experience of the Session 3 practice activity. What did you learn or experience in your efforts to be more authentic in relationships and on social media?

- What insights did you discover in the personal study or in the chapter you read from the #*Struggles* book?

- How did the last session impact your daily life or your relationship with God?

- What questions would you like to ask the other members of your group?

Video: Resurrecting Compassion (10 minutes)

Play the video segment for Session 4. As you watch, use the outline provided to follow along or to take additional notes on anything that stands out to you.

Notes

One of the problems of being selfie-centered is we often care less about other people.

There's a sharp decline in empathy. We care about 40 percent less than people did in the 1980s.

The drop in empathy also coincides with the rise in use of social media.

Three reasons we may be caring less:

1. *We are more obsessed with ourselves.*

2. *We are exposed to so much suffering that we're becoming desensitized.*

3. *Lack of personal interaction makes it easier not to care.*

True <u>compassion demands</u> action. *frustration: can't act*

To say you care but not act is to not care at all.

Caring is not clicking; it's acting.

Caring is not Liking a post; it's loving a person.

Three compassion principles:

1. *Compassion interrupts.*

    Jesus constantly allowed other people to interrupt him, and he placed their needs above his own personal agenda.

    If you are too rushed, you'll miss the blessings of God's divine interruptions.

2. *Compassion costs.*

    Drive-by compassion: I'm going to do the least and easiest thing to show that I care.

    Clicking is clean but compassion is complicated.

3. *Compassion changes lives.*

    When you get out of the selfie-centered world and start showing God's love, suddenly lives will be changed all around you.

    Not only will God change other people, but he will change you.

The closer I get to Jesus, the more I care about him, the less I care about me, and the more I care about other people.

Jesus is calling us as his disciples to show his love.

Group Discussion (36 minutes)

Take time to talk about what you just watched.

1. What part of the teaching had the most impact on you?

Caring More or Less

2. Go around the group and have each person name the issue they researched in the group opener activity (poverty, racism, refugees, etc.) and then read aloud the facts they wrote down.

    •   How do you tend to respond to this kind of information about suffering in the world? For example, do you feel overwhelmed, angry, numb, motivated to take action, avoidant, curious to learn more?

- Craig described how a constant barrage of information can lead to desensitization—we care less because we see so much. Describe how you notice this in yourself by completing this sentence: *I know I'm desensitized to information about suffering when* ...

3. A recent study demonstrated that compassion is easiest to experience when we identify with someone else and feel that we have something in common with that person:

> The compassion we feel for others is not solely a function of what befalls them: if our minds draw an association between a victim and ourselves—even a relatively trivial one—the compassion we feel for his or her suffering is amplified greatly.... Simply learning to mentally recategorize one another in terms of commonalities would generate greater empathy among all of us.[7]

Briefly review the facts you wrote down in the group opener activity. Try to imagine for a moment what it might be like to find yourself among this population—for example, to live in poverty, have experienced racism, be a refugee, etc.

- Take a moment to reflect on the impact this experience would have on your life—your emotions, your dignity, your relationships, your ability to function in life, etc. What might that be like for you?

- Now consider the ways you already relate to the experiences you just described. In your life as it is right now, what do you have in common with this population? For example, how might some aspect of your life be described as impoverished (poverty), discriminated against (racism), or forcibly displaced (refugees)?

- In what ways, if any, has this exercise of seeking commonalities impacted your ability to feel compassion in connection with the facts you discovered?

Compassion in Action

4. Craig stated that clicking is not caring—true compassion demands action. One way to think about this is to define compassion as doing for others what we would want done for us, which is precisely how Jesus summarizes what it means to put love into action:

> Do to others as you would have them do to you.
>
> (Luke 6:31)

It's a principle vividly illustrated in the story of the Good Samaritan. When an expert in Jewish religious law tried to find a loophole to justify not putting love into action, he put Jesus to the test by asking, "And who is my neighbor?" Instead of responding with an abstract definition, Jesus told a love-in-action story:

> "A Jewish man was traveling from Jerusalem down to Jericho, and he was attacked by bandits. They stripped him of his clothes, beat him up, and left him half dead beside the road.

> "By chance a priest came along. But when he saw the man lying there, he crossed to the other side of the road and passed him by. A Temple assistant walked over and looked at him lying there, but he also passed by on the other side.

> "Then a despised Samaritan came along, and when he saw the man, he felt compassion for him. Going over to him, the Samaritan soothed his wounds with olive oil and wine and bandaged them. Then he put the man on his own donkey and took him to an inn, where he took care of him. The next day he handed the innkeeper two silver coins, telling him, 'Take care of this man. If his bill runs higher than this, I'll pay you the next time I'm here.'

"Now which of these three would you say was a neighbor to the man who was attacked by bandits?" Jesus asked.

The man replied, "The one who showed him mercy."

Then Jesus said, "Yes, now go and do the same."

(Luke 10:30–37 NLT)

- All three travelers who came across the wounded man made their first decisions with their feet: the priest "crossed to the other side of the road," the temple assistant "also passed by on the other side," but the Samaritan is described as "going over to him." What parallels do you recognize between the travelers' first actions and the principle of commonality, of choosing or not choosing to identify with someone?

- The Latin root of the English word *compassion* means to "suffer with." In what ways did the Samaritan suffer with the man attacked by bandits?

- Try to reimagine the story in the context of the Internet and social media. Imagine that all the characters involved have smartphones and actively post on their own blogs or sites such as Facebook, Twitter, Instagram, etc. How do you imagine the story would play out? For example, what might each of the travelers post or not post, and how do you imagine you and others might respond to each post?

5. Craig described how compassion—putting love into action—almost always interrupts our agendas.

- Have you ever had what turned out to be a divine interruption— God prompting you to respond to something or someone that wasn't on your agenda? What happened? What might you have missed had you not allowed yourself to be interrupted?

- Author Bob Goff once tweeted, "The battle for our hearts [is] fought on the pages of our calendar. It's Thursday—quit something."[8] In other words, if the speed at which you're living makes it nearly impossible for you to at least temporarily set aside your agenda, you're not only too busy, but you're losing the battle for your heart.

  How is this battle taking place on your calendar these days? For example, in what area of your daily life are you most resistant to having your schedule or agenda interrupted?

  How willing are you to quit something—to rearrange your life and schedule to make more room for divine interruptions?

6. Clicking is clean, but compassion is both costly and complicated.

- Craig described "drive-by compassion" as doing the least and easiest thing we can do to show that we care. When are you most likely to engage in drive-by compassion?

- What kinds of things has compassion cost you over the years? What has it cost you lately?

7. It's often easy to see how compassion changes the lives of those on the receiving end—the hungry are fed, the lonely are comforted, the wounded are healed. But compassion also changes those on the giving end—the stingy become generous, the selfish become servants, the fearful become trusting.

    What changes if you think of compassion less as an isolated action and more as God's transformation plan for you—the means by which he is making you more like Jesus?

8. Touch base with each other about how you're doing in the group. Use one of the sentence starters below, or your own statement, to help group members learn more about how to be good friends to you.

    I want to give you permission to challenge me more about ...

    An area where I really need your help or sensitivity is ...

    It always helps me to feel more connected to the group when ...

    Something I've learned about myself because of this group is ...

Individual Activity: What I Want to Remember (2 minutes)

Complete this activity on your own.

1. Briefly review the outline and any notes you took.

2. In the space below, write down the most significant thing you gained in this session — from the teaching, activities, or discussions.

   What I want to remember from this session ...

Practice: iCare

The practice for this week is to pursue compassion by putting love into action. Choose one or more of the following options as your practice between now and the next group meeting.

❏ *Learn more.* Take the topic you identified at the beginning of the session (or choose another topic that interests you) and deepen your knowledge about the complexities of that issue. Use the six basic questions of information gathering — who, what, when, where, why, how — to write up a one-page summary of what you learn. In addition to getting the facts, put a human face on what you learn by gathering any stories you can find of those who are affected. Identify local, national, and/or international organizations devoted to compassionate engagement and response. If possible and appropriate, seek to have a conversation with someone locally to learn more. For example, you might talk with a staff person, a volunteer, or a resident at a local homeless shelter. Use what you learn to identify at least one way you can put love into action before the next group session.

❏ *Pray for divine interruptions.* Author Bob Goff writes, "Loving people the way Jesus did means living a life of constant interruptions. Bring it."* Rather than trying to avoid interruptions, take the initiative and ask God to send them your way each day. Change your default mode from a bias toward "no" to a bias toward "yes." (If you have people-pleasing tendencies and already say yes too often, take a pass on this one; it's not for you!) The invitation here is to practice saying an empowered yes instead of a defensive no when unexpected opportunities to love — interruptions — come your way. Be open to yeses of any size — small, medium, or large.

Use a pad of paper or your journal to keep a daily list of your divine interruptions and your responses. If you miss opportunities to say yes, that's okay. God is happy for you to try again the next day.

❑ *Sponsor a vulnerable child.* For a monthly donation (typically less than forty dollars), many Christian organizations and denominations provide holistic aid to children that includes nutrition, mentoring, medical checkups, educational assistance, and more. Examples include Compassion International (compassion.com), World Vision (worldvision.org), and Food for the Hungry (fh.org). Visit websites, read stories, and see photos of children all over the world who are waiting for sponsors. Choose a child to sponsor, and commit your heart as well as your monthly financial support to his or her well-being. Learn more about the country and the circumstances in which your child lives, place his or her photo in a prominent place in your home where you will see it often, and pray for your child daily.

❑ *Make a sacrificial gift.* Choose to forgo something you planned to spend money on in order to spend or give that money to make a difference in someone else's life. Or, give a gift of your time — an hour, an afternoon, a whole day — to serve others, to invest in someone, or simply to spend time with someone who could use a listening ear and a compassionate presence. Whatever your gift, seek to give it with your whole heart, not out of obligation or duty but as an expression of your love for Christ.

Place a check mark next to one or more of the options you'll practice this week and share it with the group.

Whichever option(s) you choose, consider setting aside some time to write down a few notes and observations about your experience throughout the week. You'll have a chance to talk about your experiences at the start of Session 5.

---

*Bob Goff, @bobgoff (3 October 2014) Tweet.

Closing Prayer

Close your time together with prayer. Following prayer, retrieve your electronic devices.

Get a Head Start on the Discussion for Session 5

As part of the group discussion for Session 5, you'll have an opportunity to talk about what you've learned and experienced together throughout the #*Struggles* study. Between now and your next meeting, take a few moments to review the previous sessions and identify the teaching, discussions, or insights that stand out most to you. Use the worksheet on the following pages to briefly summarize the highlights of what you've learned and experienced.

Session 5 Head Start Worksheet

Take a few moments to reflect on what you've learned and experienced throughout the #*Struggles* study. You may want to review notes from the video teaching, what you wrote down for "What I Want to Remember" at the end of each group session, responses in the personal studies, etc. Here are some questions you might consider as part of your review:

- What insights did I gain from this session?

- What was the most important thing I learned about myself in this session?

- How did I experience God's presence or leading related to this session?

- How did this session impact my relationships with the other people in the group?

Use the spaces provided below and on the next page to briefly summarize what you've learned and experienced for each session.

Session 1: Recovering Contentment

Session 2: Restoring Intimacy

Session 3: Revealing Authenticity

Session 4: Resurrecting Compassion

#4

Personal Study

Read and Learn

Read chapter 4 of #*Struggles*. Use the space below to note any insights or questions you want to bring to the next group session.

Study and Reflect

Here's something I know for a fact: when people are really close to Jesus, their life becomes no longer about themselves. It becomes about glorifying God and loving others.

#*Struggles*, page 99

1. God's hope for us is not that we become accomplished at checking off items on a long to-do list of compassionate actions but that we are transformed into persons from whom compassion naturally flows. In order for compassion to move from "what I do" to "who I am," we need to be close to Jesus, continually renewed and transformed by his love. Author and pastor Peter Scazzero writes:

    > The love of Jesus in you is the greatest gift you have to give others. Period. Who you are as a person—and specifically how well you love—will always have a larger and longer impact on those around you than what you do. Your being with God (or lack of being with God) will trump, eventually, your doing for God every time. We cannot give what we do not possess.[9]

    Overall, how would you describe where you are when it comes to compassion? Does it feel more like "what you do" or more like "who you are"? Place an X on the continuum to indicate your response.

    ●————————————————————————————————●

Compassion Is What I Do	Compassion Is Who I Am
My doing for Jesus flows out of my own efforts and/or my desire to earn his love.	My doing for Jesus flows out of my being with Jesus and receiving his love.

    If you placed your X closer to the right, what practices, experiences, or relationships enable you to receive and rely on Christ's love for you? If you placed your X closer to the left, what issues or challenges make it difficult for you to receive and rely on Christ's love for you?

    Based on your relationship with Jesus, how would you describe your capacity for extending compassion to others right now? For example, do you have a little love to give, a lot, or somewhere inbetween? Are you able to extend compassion to most or just a few?

In what area of your life are you especially aware of needing to be with Jesus—to receive more of his compassionate love for you?

2. Jesus used the metaphor of a vine and branches to describe the vital connection between remaining in his love and our ability to live a fruitful life of loving others. Read the following passage slowly, underlining any words or phrases that stand out to you.

> Remain in me, as I also remain in you. No branch can bear fruit by itself; it must remain in the vine. Neither can you bear fruit unless you remain in me.

> I am the vine; you are the branches. If you remain in me and I in you, you will bear much fruit; apart from me you can do nothing. If you do not remain in me, you are like a branch that is thrown away and withers; such branches are picked up, thrown into the fire and burned....

> As the Father has loved me, so have I loved you. Now remain in my love. If you keep my commands, you will remain in my love, just as I have kept my Father's commands and remain in his love. I have told you this so that my joy may be in you and that your joy may be complete. My command is this: Love each other as I have loved you.

> (John 15:4–6, 9–12)

Now read the passage again, this time from *The Message*:

> Live in me. Make your home in me just as I do in you. In the same way that a branch can't bear grapes by itself but only by being joined to the vine, you can't bear fruit unless you are joined with me.

> I am the Vine, you are the branches. When you're joined with me and I with you, the relation intimate and organic, the harvest is sure to be abundant. Separated, you can't produce a thing. Anyone who separates from me is deadwood, gathered up and thrown on the bonfire....

> I've loved you the way my Father has loved me. Make yourselves at home in my love. If you keep my commands, you'll remain intimately at home in my love. That's what I've done—kept my

Father's commands and made myself at home in his love. I've told you these things for a purpose: that my joy might be your joy, and your joy wholly mature. This is my command: Love one another the way I loved you.

(John 15:4–6, 9–12 MSG)

Jesus makes repeated use of the word *remain* to describe the intimate nature of the relationships between the Father, himself, and his followers. But the foundational "remain"—the *first* thing Jesus asks us to do—is to remain in him by allowing ourselves to be loved.

If Jesus' love for you is the foundation for everything he asks you to do, how does it impact your view of obedience, of keeping Christ's commands? For example, when Jesus presents you with an opportunity to love, what if the foundational question he's really asking is, "Will you allow me to love you in this way?"

In what ways or in what areas of life do you struggle to "remain" in Christ—to be at home in his love?

What parallels or connections might exist between your struggle to be at home in Christ's love and the ways in which you sometimes struggle to show compassionate love to others?

The choice to remain—to let Jesus love us—brings with it two promises: that we will bear much fruit and that our joy will be complete. What fears and/or hopes come to mind when you consider that these promises are not just for Jesus' followers in general but for you specifically?

How do you sense Jesus may be inviting you to remain with him, to make your home in his love this day?

3.   Read Psalm 103, a psalm of David that praises God for all of the ways he has demonstrated his compassionate love. Drawing on the psalm as a reference, use the space below to write your own prayer of praise to God. Express your gratitude for all the ways he has been compassionate and gracious to you. Confess any ways in which you may have separated yourself from his love, asking for whatever it is you need from him to help you remain in his love this day. Ask God to make you fruitful in extending his compassionate love to others—to family and friends as well as to any divine interruptions he may bring your way.

#5

replenishing rest

The Struggle with Constant Distraction

> The soul craves rest. Our wills sometimes rejoice in striving; our bodies were made to (at least some times) know the exhilaration of tremendous challenge; our minds get stretched when they must focus even when tired. But the soul craves rest. The soul knows only borrowed strength. The soul was made to rest in God the way a tree rests in soil.
>
> John Ortberg, *Soul Keeping*

Group Activity: Devices Out and Away (2 minutes)

Welcome to Session 5 of #*Struggles*. In this session, we'll consider how technology and social media impact the ability of our souls to be at rest. Once again, you'll continue to build on the practice of separating yourself from your electronics for the duration of your group meeting.

1. Take out your phone, tablet, or any other electronic device you may have with you. Turn it off or place it in airplane mode.

2. Choose a container such as a small box, basket, or a shopping bag and have everyone place their devices in the container. Place the container out of sight—in a cabinet, closet, or nearby room.

3. Continue with the remainder of the group meeting. Retrieve your devices after closing prayer at the end of the meeting.

Group Discussion: Checking In (5 minutes)

Check in with each other about what you've learned and experienced since the last session. For example:

- Briefly share your experience of the Session 4 practice activity. What did you learn or experience in your efforts to demonstrate compassionate love?

- What insights did you discover in the personal study or in the chapter you read from the #*Struggles* book?

- How did the last session impact your daily life or your relationship with God?

- What questions would you like to ask the other members of your group?

Video: Replenishing Rest (10 minutes)

Play the video segment for Session 5. As you watch, use the outline provided to follow along or to take additional notes on anything that stands out to you.

Notes

"I love technology, but at the same time, I hate it."

"'I have the right to do anything,' you say—but not everything is beneficial. 'I have the right to do anything'—but I will not be mastered by anything" (1 Corinthians 6:12).

Nomophobia is the fear of being away from mobile devices.

Fifty-eight percent of people don't go one waking hour without checking their phone.

Eighty-four percent of people say they couldn't go one day without their phone.

We are unable to shut down on the inside. Our brains are always running.

We need to recognize that our souls need rest.

God has a very special rest for us in Christ.

"Come to me, all you who are weary and burdened, and I will give you rest. Take my yoke upon you and learn from me, for I am gentle and humble in heart, and you will find rest for your souls" (Matthew 11:28–29).

Two ways to experience deep soul rest in God.

1. *Learn to be still.*

"Be still, and know that I am God" (Psalm 46:10).

"But I have stilled and quieted my soul, like a weaned child with its mother, like a weaned child is my soul within me" (Psalm 131:2 NIV 1984).

You don't have time not to be still. Learn to be still in the presence of God.

2. *Make a plan.*

"A wise man thinks ahead; a fool doesn't and even brags about it!" (Proverbs 13:16 TLB).

Any plan needs a good defense and a good offense.

Defense: Strategies we put into place to protect ourselves

Offense: Actions we take to travel where we believe God wants us to go

Has technology taken a place of idolatry in your heart?

"This is what the LORD says: Stand at the crossroads and look; ask for the ancient paths, ask where the good way is, and walk in it, and you will find rest for your souls" (Jeremiah 6:16).

Group Discussion (41 minutes)

Take time to talk about what you just watched.

1. What part of the teaching had the most impact on you?

Fear and Fatigue

2. Craig described how many people experience nomophobia, which is a fear of being separated from mobile devices.

    *   Describe the range of things you're afraid might happen if you are separated from your device. What are the small things and what is the worst-case scenario?

    *   What is the worst thing that has actually happened as a result of being separated from your device?

3. Mobile technology is a powerful tool that puts the world at our fingertips. It gives us instant access to knowledge, makes us powerful in ways unknown to previous generations, and enables us to be virtually present almost anywhere in the world without ever leaving home. To a degree, our devices allow us to feel omniscient, omnipotent, and omnipresent—the three attributes uniquely characteristic of God alone. God is:

    Omniscient, which means all-knowing. God knows the past, the present, and the future. Nothing takes God by surprise.

Omnipotent, which means all-powerful. God is not subject to limitations in the natural or supernatural world.

Omnipresent, which means all-present. God is everywhere, at the same time, always.

- Which of the three attributes comes closest to describing the way you rely on your phone most? For example, "I want to be omnipresent. I rely on my phone most to help me be multiple places at the same time."

- In what ways does your device give you the illusion of feeling powerful or in control when it comes to the fears you identified in question 2? For example, "If I'm reachable, I can prevent my child from being harmed," or "If I stay current, I'll never miss out or be caught off guard."

- How does this idea that our devices give us the illusion of godlike control explain why they might also leave us with soul fatigue?

Be Still

4. Craig described how we can begin to give our souls rest when we learn to be still in God's presence. With the psalmist, we receive the Lord's invitation to, "Be still, and know that I am God" (Psalm 46:10). One of the ways we can learn to be still is to practice the spiritual discipline of silence. Author and pastor Adele Calhoun writes:

> The discipline of silence invites us to leave behind the competing demands of our outer world for time alone with Jesus. Silence offers a way of paying attention to the Spirit of God and what he brings to the surface of our souls.... Silence is a time to rest in God. Lean into God, trusting that being with him in silence will loosen your rootedness in the world and plant you by streams of living water.[10]

What's your response to this kind of silent resting in God? Is it something you feel resistant to or something that you feel drawn to? Share the reasons for your response.

5. Use the following activity to practice silence and be still together in God's presence.

Group Activity

a. Appoint one person with a watch to be timekeeper.

b. Set aside your study materials so your hands and lap are empty, and then settle into a comfortable position.

c. Spend five minutes together in silence. As you begin, you may wish to close your eyes, inhale deeply, and exhale slowly. Silently ask God to help you rest in him.

d. When five minutes have passed, the timekeeper closes your time of silence by saying, "Amen."

Group Discussion

• How did you experience the five minutes? Did it seem long or did it go by too quickly for you?

• What were you aware of in the silence? For example, did a thousand thoughts rush through your mind? Did you notice any particular emotions? In what ways, if any, did you experience rest?

6. Take a few moments to discuss what you've learned and experienced together throughout the *#Struggles* study.

    *   What would you say is the most important thing you learned or experienced? How has it impacted you? For example: in what ways, if any, has it changed how you view or use technology and social media?

    *   How did your experience of being separated from your phone during group time change over the course of the study? For example: did you find it easier to let it go from one week to the next?

    *   How else have you recognized God at work in your life through the study?

    *   How have you recognized God's work among you in the group?

Individual Activity: What I Want to Remember (2 minutes)

Complete this activity on your own.

1. Briefly review the outline and any notes you took.

2. In the space below, write down the most significant thing you gained in this session — from the teaching, activities, or discussions.

   What I want to remember from this session . . .

Practice: iRest

The practice for this week is to make room in our lives for rest by being still in God's presence and putting boundaries on technology. Choose one or more of the following options as your practice for the week ahead.

❑ *Practice silence daily.* Set aside time each day to be still and rest in God's presence. Find a quiet place where you won't be interrupted and settle into a comfortable position. You may wish to set a timer for five to ten minutes to avoid being distracted about how much time has passed. Begin by inviting God to be with you. You might pray, "Come, Holy Spirit," or "Jesus, help me to be present with you." Then rest quietly in silence, trusting that the Lord is with you and longs to give you rest. Whatever the outcome, resist the temptation to judge your time in silence as a success or failure. God is pleased even by your desire to spend time with him.

❑ *Make a plan.* Making time to quiet your soul requires a plan, and every good plan requires a good defense and a good offense.

  • *Defense.* Your defense is the strategies you put in place to protect yourself. Identify the ways in which you sense technology or social media may be mastering you rather than you mastering it (1 Corinthians 6:12). Then set the ground rules and boundaries that will protect you and put you in the power position. For example: ask your family to join you in silencing phones during meals; put your phone away an hour before bed and don't check it again until after breakfast in the morning; turn off social media notifications; give your phone to someone else when you need to concentrate at work; limit social media consumption to once a day; designate a day or more each week as a social media break. Your defense can be virtually anything that puts you back in charge and protects you from being distracted and consumed by technology.

- *Offense.* Your offense is the actions you take to travel where you believe God wants you to go. Consider again the ways in which you want to be the master of your technology and to experience rest. What will get you there? For example, commit to a consistent, focused prayer time in which you ask God to lead you and then spend time listening for his guidance. You may need to focus on nondigital forms of entertainment, such as reading a printed book, spending time outside in nature, or playing games that come in a box rather than a device. Watch a sunset or spend time with friends without thinking of how you can capture the experience for social media. Ask friends and family to help you build richness into your relational life with activities that don't require electronics.

For additional ideas to help you develop your plan, see "The Ten Commandments for Using Social Media to Grow Your Faith and Share God's Love" in the back of this study guide.

Put your plan in writing and share it with your family or a close friend, asking for their support. Review it at the beginning or end of each day as a reminder of your commitments.

❑ *Take a cyber Sabbath.* Biblical Sabbath is a weekly day of complete rest. It commemorates the day God rested after his work in creation (Exodus 20:8–11), and also the gift of rest God gave to the Israelites after they were released from four hundred years of slavery in Egypt. In the Jewish tradition, Sabbath is a twenty-four-hour period that begins at sunset on Friday evening and concludes with sunset on Saturday. To take a cyber Sabbath, choose a twenty-four-hour period in which you will rest from all electronics. As a courtesy, you may wish to alert those close to you about your cyber Sabbath plans and also put an auto-response on email or a post on social media to let others know you're taking a twenty-four-hour break. If you rely on your devices for information or entertainment, make a plan a few days ahead for how you will spend your time on your Sabbath so you can make arrangements in advance for anything you may need to know. Do your creative best to protect the day from technology "cheats" so that you can rest from distraction and your dependence on electronics.

Place a check mark next to one or more of the options you'll practice this week and share it with the group.

Whichever option(s) you choose, consider setting aside some time to write down a few notes and observations about your experience throughout the week. If your group is ongoing, allow time at your next gathering to talk about your experiences of rest. If this is your last group meeting, commit to sharing your experience with a friend or another member of the group one-on-one.

Closing Prayer

Close your time together with prayer. Following prayer, retrieve your electronic devices.

#5

Personal Study

Read and Learn

Read chapter 8 of #*Struggles*. Use the space below to note any insights or questions you have.

Study and Reflect

We're constantly distracted. We can't work productively for long stretches because we allow something to ping or beep and break our concentration. We let our RPMs run all the time, constantly revving our mental and emotional engines. We feel overwhelmed, and we don't know why. We're short with our children, and we don't know why. We feel exhausted spiritually, and we don't know why. We long for something more. Ironically, we keep returning to the source of our discontent, and of course we won't find peace there.

Something has to change.

#Struggles, page 180

1. Take a moment to imagine an ordinary day without technology, social media, or the Internet. Although there would definitely be inconveniences, focus your attention instead on the loss of distractions and how you might otherwise use time that would have been spent engaged with a device (phone, iPod, tablet, laptop, handheld electronic games, etc.).

> **Example**
>
> Morning routine ... *I wouldn't be checking my email or news sites while simultaneously trying to get ready and eat breakfast, so I might be less rushed. Walking to the train station, I wouldn't be wearing my earphones, so I'd likely be paying more attention to what's happening around me. On the train, instead of listening to the radio on my phone while checking Facebook and email, I'd probably enjoy reading a book or a magazine.*

Morning routine ...

Meal times ...

Work/school (meetings, tasks, classes, studying) ...

Between times (waiting, walking between locations, transitions between events or commitments) ...

Free time or entertainment ...

Time with friends/family ...

Exercise ...

Evening routine ...

Other ...

Briefly review your responses. After imagining a day without technology, how would you say technology contributes to "revving your mental and emotional engines"? How does it multiply distractions or add to your sense of fatigue?

> Sometimes we just have to tell our soul to chill. "Cool it, soul. Don't get so wound up. Sit down. Rest. Take a breather."
>
> #*Struggles*, page 183

2. Scripture offers a beautiful contrast to soul fatigue in the image the psalmist uses to describe his soul at rest:

    > But I have stilled and quieted my soul; like a weaned child with its mother, like a weaned child is my soul within me. (Psalm 131:2 NIV 1984)

    Notice the psalmist indicates it's possible to choose to do this. His soul wasn't just calmed somehow by accident. He stilled and quieted it himself.

    The Hebrew word used for *stilled* means "to soothe," but it is also used to describe the process of making something smooth, level, or equal,[11] as in leveling ground.[12]

    The Hebrew word used for *quieted* means "to be motionless and silent." One Bible scholar describes it as "the silence of trust."[13] The image overall is that of a trusting child whose needs have been met and is content to rest and be quietly held.

If you imagine your soul as a small child, how would you describe it? What condition is it in? What does it most need?

Take a few minutes now to still and quiet your soul as the psalmist did. Allow yourself to be a child in God's presence, to rest and be quietly held. If time is a concern, set a timer for five to ten minutes.

Settle into a comfortable position. Inhale deeply and exhale slowly. Invite God to be with you. You might pray, "Come, Holy Spirit," or "Here I am, Lord." Rest quietly in silence, trusting that God is with you and that he knows what you need.

After concluding your time of silence, use the questions below to reflect on your experience.

What were you most aware of as you were quiet?

In what ways did God seem present or absent?

What hindered or helped your soul to rest?

3. Read Psalm 23, a beloved prayer expressing trust in the Good Shep-
    herd who refreshes our souls. Drawing on the psalm as a reference,
    use the space below to write your own prayer. Share the condition of
    your soul, including your depletion, fears, and needs, and ask God
    to provide what you need. Affirm your trust in him and thank him for
    the promise of green pastures and quiet waters where your soul can
    rest safely in him.

The Ten Commandments for Using Social Media to Grow Your Faith and Share God's Love

Here are ten ways you can protect your time, your heart, your body, and your soul, as well as deepen your faith through what you type, text, and tweet. Social media and technology are amazing tools, and with a little discipline and prayer, they can be a gift to connect with others and reflect your love for an amazing God.

1. Put God First in All You Say and Post.

The apostle Paul says it clearly: "And whatever you do, whether in word or deed, do it all in the name of the Lord Jesus, giving thanks to God the Father through him" (Colossians 3:17). Because our lives belong to God, he should be first in all we do. We could translate this into our social-media culture by saying: "Whatever you do, whether tweeting, commenting, posting, or uploading, do it all in the name of the Lord Jesus."

Before saying anything online (or in person), ask yourself whether you are truly representing and reflecting the love and goodness of God. If not, don't say it. Ever. And don't just think about the words you say; think about the pictures or videos you post. If in any way they don't reflect God's standards, don't share them.

2. Love Others as You Want to Be Loved.

When you think about how you like to be loved online, it's easy to know how to treat others. You can Like someone's post. You can retweet what they say or reply with a kind word or two. You can offer a sincere and uplifting compliment. You can comment positively on something they said or posted.

Likewise, you can refrain from saying something hurtful to others, being antagonistic, or always ignoring what they do or say. This doesn't mean that we avoid tough issues. But we can talk about them from a positive perspective, offering solutions rather than poking at people and making others look bad.

You know tons of things that people do for you that help you feel loved. So get creative online and off and love others in the same ways you want to be loved!

3. Use Social Media to Facilitate, Not Replace, Real Relationships.

We should maximize all that technology offers to help strengthen our friendships and relationships. But as the gravitational pull to live online continues to grow, we must remind ourselves that the best relationships are not those that are limited to looking at a screen but those that involve loving an actual person in person.

So text away. Tweet what you're doing. Post what you're eating. But put more effort into your treasured relationships. Remember to call. Plan a visit. Eat with someone, and then sit and chat for two hours afterward. Sit across from each other in a coffee shop and talk about everything that matters and a few things that don't. Make a meal for someone and bring it to their house. Take a long walk with a friend and just chat about whatever comes to mind. When someone you love is injured and in the hospital, don't just text them; go visit them. Don't just do life together from a distance. Do life up close. As Paul might have tweeted, "Be devoted to one another in love" (Romans 12:10).

4. Use Social Media Instead of Being Controlled by It as an Idol.

As followers of Jesus, we need to make sure a good thing never becomes a supreme thing. Unquestionably, leveraging technology to share about Jesus and to connect with people is a good thing. But if left unchecked, using technology can become obsessive and idolatrous.

It's hard to see in the moment, but when we stand back, we realize that we might as well have bowed down before a giant smartphone in the sky. The Bible couldn't be clearer about idolatry. In addition to the commandment to "have no other gods before me" (Exodus 20:3), we're also told: "Dear children, keep yourselves from idols" (1 John 5:21). As soon as you realize that you don't have control—that you click and click again without knowing how to stop—acknowledge the problem. Don't rationalize it. Don't explain it away. And don't put off dealing with it.

5. Turn Your Virtual Other Cheek to Posts That Offend You.

Follow enough people, and it won't take long: someone will say or show something inappropriate or offensive. If you're like most people, you find it easy to get up in arms and take offense. As Christians, though, we can rise above the temptation to get down in the dirt. Solomon says, "A person's wisdom yields patience; it is to one's glory to *overlook an offense*" (Proverbs 19:11, emphasis added). To be clear, overlooking an offense isn't the same as pretending it didn't happen or encouraging injustice. No, to overlook something is a decision to let it go. It's a form of forgiveness.

If a post starts to grieve your heart or make you unrighteously angry, remember that you don't have to follow the post-er. You can to some degree control what you see and read. No matter what, remember that just as Jesus taught us to turn the other cheek when someone strikes us, so we can turn a virtual other cheek to posts that offend us (Matthew 5:39).

6. Do Not Post Out of Emotion.

When you think about it, the ability to say whatever you're thinking to a large group of semi-interested people is pretty scary, which is a good reason to never post when you're feeling angry, upset, rejected, or offended, or battling any other unsettling emotions. If you're wondering whether or not you are responding out of emotion, remember this: when in doubt, wait it out. Without a doubt, you will be tempted to post when you're agitated or hurt. But when in doubt, hold off until you can respond sensibly. Post only out of love.

7. Always Reflect Jesus, Loving God Whether Online or Off.

Above all else, the most important command we have is to love God with every part of our being (Matthew 22:37–38). Therefore, we should always love and reflect Jesus online and off.

I encourage you to go through everything you've posted or said online in the past month. Pretend as if you don't know anything about yourself and determine what conclusions someone would draw about you based on what you've posted. Does what you show accurately reflect what you believe? Would people say you love God above all? Or would they think you love something else more—maybe even yourself? If this evidence is not in your posts, ask yourself why not. Are you afraid of what people will think? Or worse yet, are you revealing that you aren't really loving God above all else?

If you are falling more and more in love with God each day, your love will show in the things you post. You won't have to force it or fake it.

8. Do Not Use Social Media to Fuel Temptations.

It's no secret that technology and social media can open the door to temptations with simple clicks or keystrokes. Instead of having to go through numerous steps, actions, or behaviors to come face-to-face with a fierce temptation, we can now encounter it on our monitor in nanoseconds.

As a believer in Jesus, you never have to battle temptation alone. The author of Hebrews reminds us, "Because [Jesus] himself suffered when he was tempted, he is able to help those who are being tempted" (Hebrews 2:18). If you are being tempted, you are not on your own. Jesus is able to help you. So if you spot an open door to online temptation, ask Jesus to help you close it. When he shows you how to shut the door to online temptation, slam that door, lock it, and throw away the encryption key. Delete the app if you have to. Or if you need to, give someone else a password to keep yourself from having access to download apps. You might need to download a filtered browser or block certain websites. Or you might share passwords or have joint accounts with your spouse. Whatever it takes, thou shalt not use technology to fuel temptation.

9. Form Your Own Opinions; Do Not Follow the Crowd.

When you follow other people online, you can learn a lot of wisdom from those who are wise. Unfortunately, some people are not only *not* wise, but they can be downright foolish.

Often on social media, many people jump on the bandwagons of opinions about God, politics, or the latest celebrity scandal. However, just because a lot of people believe something doesn't make it true, especially when it comes to what people post online.

It may be tempting to follow the crowd, but doing so can be dangerous. Exodus 23:2 says, "Do not follow the crowd in doing wrong." God gave you a brain to think for yourself. He gave you his Word to seek his will. He gave you his Spirit to guide you into all truth (see John 16:13). Instead of believing everything you see or hear, think for yourself.

10. Do Not Base Your Identity on What People Think.

Anyone who spends time on social media will be tempted to compare, thinking, "How many followers do they have? Wow! That's way more than I have." We may also be tempted to think the opposite when we see that someone gets fewer Likes or mentions than we do—that they aren't as important as we are. An unhealthy view of social media can cause us to feel either an ungodly pride or an unhealthy sense of inadequacy.

As Christians, we must constantly remind ourselves not to base our identity—our view of ourselves and our worth—on what other people say or think about us. Who we are and our value is determined by what Christ says about us. Others may criticize us, ignore us, or unfollow us, but that doesn't affect who we really are. We are who Christ says we are.

Notes

1. Os Guinness, *The Call: Finding and Fulfilling the Central Purpose of Your Life* (Nashville: W Publishing Group, 1998, 2003), 124.

2. Andrew K. Przybylski and Netta Weinstein, "Can You Connect with Me Now? How the Presence of Mobile Communication Technology Influences Face-to-Face Conversation Quality," *Journal of Social and Personal Relationships,* May 2013, vol. 30, no. 3, 237–246.

3. Jean Vanier, *Seeing Beyond Depression* (Mahwah, N.J.: Paulist Press, 2001), 19.

4. Brené Brown, accessed July 6, 2015, brenebrown.com/downloads-badges/.

5. Colin Brown, "Parable," *New International Dictionary of New Testament Theology*, vol. 2, Colin Brown, gen. ed. (Grand Rapids: Zondervan, 1976, 1986), 756.

6. Frederick Buechner, *Telling Secrets: A Memoir* (SanFrancisco: HarperSanFrancisco, 1991), 2–3.

7. Dr. David DeSteno, "Compassion Made Easy," *New York Times*, July 14, 2012, accessed online July 6, 2015.

8. Bob Goff, @bobgoff (4 April 2013) Tweet.

9. Peter Scazzero, *The Emotionally Healthy Leader: How Transforming Your Inner Life Will Deeply Transform Your Church, Team, and the World* (Grand Rapids: Zondervan, 2015), 40.

10. Adele Ahlberg Calhoun, *Spiritual Disciplines Handbook: Practices That Transform Us* (Downers Grove, Ill.: InterVarsity Press, 2005), 108–109.

11. Louis Jonker, "sawâhl," *New International Dictionary of Old Testament Theology and Exegesis*, vol. 4, Willem A. VanGemeren, gen. ed. (Grand Rapids: Zondervan, 1997), 59.

12. Leslie C. Allen, *Word Biblical Commentary: Psalms 101–150*, vol. 21, Ralph P. Martin, ed. (Nashville: Thomas Nelson, 2002), 259.

13. John N. Oswalt, "de mâmâ," *New International Dictionary of Old Testament Theology and Exegesis*, vol. 1, Willem A. VanGemeren, gen. ed. (Grand Rapids: Zondervan, 1997), 972.

#Struggles
Following Jesus in a Selfie-Centered World

Craig Groeschel

We all love the benefits of technology and social media, but even with the incredible upsides, many of us suspect there are unintended negative consequences that are beyond our control. We've lost perspective, even perhaps ourselves.

In this timely and life-changing new book, *New York Times* best-selling author and pastor of LifeChurch.tv Craig Groeschel encourages readers who are hungry to regain control over their lives and put Christ first again. He walks them through biblical values that all Christ followers know are essential, but are even more important for our maxed out, selfie-centered world.

The more you compare, the less satisfied you are. The more we interact online, the more we crave face to face intimacy, but the harder it is to find. The more filtered our lives become, the more challenging it is to be authentic. The more information about the pain in the world we're exposed to the more difficult it is to care.

It's time to refresh and rediscover our understanding of the biblical principles that life with Christ brings: contentment, intimacy, authenticity, compassion, rest, and more. Groeschel taps in to some of the most up-to-date studies on the effects of social media on our emotions and our friendships. And he offers real-life examples of how we struggle with social media, how it masks our real struggles, and how we can reclaim a Christ-centered life.

Available in stores and online!

From This Day Forward

Five Commitments to Fail-Proof Your Marriage

Craig and Amy Groeschel

You know the stats, and they are horrifying. Fifty percent of marriages don't make it. With those kinds of odds, is it even possible to have a great marriage? Craig Groeschel insists it is so, but not if you approach it like everyone else does.

In this groundbreaking new book, *New York Times* bestselling author and pastor Craig Groeschel and his wife Amy show engaged and married couples how to conquer the odds in a culture where "I do" doesn't necessarily mean forever. This book will help you find the joy, passion, and strength of a marriage built by God. Craig and Amy present the five commitments all spouses need to make in order to absolutely fail-proof their marriage. Starting right now — from this day forward.

Small Group Curriculum Also Available:
- 5-Session DVD
- Study Guide
- Study Guide with DVD

Available in stores and online!

Fight

Winning the Battles That Matter Most

Craig Groeschel

Author and pastor Craig Groeschel helps you uncover who you really are — a man created in the image of God with a warrior's heart — and how to fight the good fight for what's right. You will find the strength to fight the battles you know you need to fight — the ones that determine the state of your heart, the quality of your marriage, and the spiritual health of your family.

Craig will also look at examples from the Bible, including our good buddy Samson. Yep, the dude with the rippling biceps, hippie hair, and a thing for Delilah. You may be surprised how much we have in common with this guy. By looking at his life, you'll learn how to defeat the demons that make strong men weak. You'll become who God made you to be:

A man who knows how to fight for what's right.

And don't you dare show up for this fight unarmed. Learn how to fight with faith, with prayer, and with the Word of God

It's time to fight like a man. For God's Sake, FIGHT.

Small Group Curriculum Also Available:
• 5-Session DVD
• Study Guide
• Study Guide with DVD

Available in stores and online!

Altar Ego

Becoming Who God Says You Are

Craig Groeschel

You are NOT who you think you are. In fact, according to bestselling author Craig Groeschel, you need to take your idea of your own identity, lay it down on the altar, and sacrifice it. Give it to God. Offer it up.

Why? Because you are who GOD says you are. And until you've sacrificed your broken concept of your identity, you won't become who you are meant to be.

When we place our false labels and self-deception on the altar of God's truth, we discover who we really are as his sons and daughters. Instead of an outward-driven, approval-based ego, we learn to live with an "altar" ego, God's vision of who we are becoming.

Discover how to trade in your broken ego and unleash your altar ego to become a living sacrifice. Once we know our true identity and are growing in Christlike character, then we can behave accordingly, with bold behavior, bold prayers, bold words, and bold obedience.

Altar Ego reveals who God says you are, and then calls you to live up to it.

Small Group Curriculum Also Available:
• 5-Session DVD
• Study Guide
• Study Guide with DVD

Available in stores and online!

More Popular DVD Studies from Craig Groeschel

Soul Detox

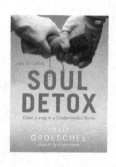

Sessions include:

1. **Lethal Language:** Experiencing the Power of Life-Giving Words
2. **Scare Pollution:** Unlocking the Chokehold of Fear
3. **Radioactive Relationships:** Loving Unhealthy People without Getting Sick
4. **Septic Thoughts:** Overcoming Our False Beliefs
5. **Germ Warfare:** Cleansing Our Lives of Cultural Toxins

Weird

Sessions include:

1. *The God Kind of Weird*
2. *It's Time to Be Weird*
3. *Weird That Money Can't Buy*
4. *Pleasing God Is Weird*
5. *Weird Makes You Truly Sexy*
6. *The Weirdest Blessing Possible*

The Christian Atheist

Sessions include:

1. *When You Believe in God but Don't Really Know Him*
2. *When You Believe in God but Don't Think He's Fair*
3. *When You Believe in God but Aren't Sure He Loves You*
4. *When You Believe in God but Trust More in Money*
5. *When You Believe in God but Pursue Happiness at Any Cost*
6. *When You Believe in God but Don't Want to Go Overboard*